ICNC **MONOGRAPH** SERIES

Nonviolent Movements and Material Resources in Northwest Mexico

Chris Allan and A. Scott DuPree

Table of Contents

Executive Summary 1

Introduction 3

    Why Are Material Resources Important to Strengthening Civil Resistance Movements? . . 3

        Material Resource Mobilization in Civil Resistance Studies 5

        The Meaning of Material Resources 9

        Philanthropic Support 10

        Types of Resources and Virtuous Cycle of Resource Mobilization 11

        The Monograph's Questions 14

        Methods Deployed 15

        Data Limitations and Protecting Privacy 15

1. Comparing the Three Movements 17

    How Do Movements Generate Material Resources,
and How Do They Decide How to Allocate Their Resources? 17

        What Resources Did They Generate? 17

        Were There Any Resources Refused or That Had Negative Consequences? 25

    What Capabilities Do Movements Need to Be Effective at Raising,
Generating, and Deploying Material Resources? 25

    What Is the Impact of the Way Material Resources Are Allocated
and Used on the Movement's Chances of Success or Failure? 28

2. The Free San Pedro River Movement, Nayarit 33

    Overview of the Movement 33

        The Seed of the Movement 33

        Growing Resistance Through Dialogue 34

    How Material Resources Were Mobilized and Used by the Movement 40

        Community Dialogues 43

        Publicity, Declarations, and Petitions 44

        Public Marches and Demonstrations 46

    Conclusions 48

3. Movement Against Toxic Mining, Baja California Sur **50**
    Overview of the Movement. **50**
        Gold Mining in the State. **50**
        The Consolidation of Resistance **51**
        Movement's Strategies to Expose Wrongdoing **52**
        Apex of Civil Resistance. **53**
        Intervention by the Courts **55**
    How Material Resources Were Mobilized and Used by the Movement **56**
        Publicizing Dissent **58**
        Blockade of Roads and Occupation of Airports **60**
    Conclusions. **61**

4. Aquí ¡No!: Stopping an Ammonia Plant, Sinaloa. **63**
    Overview of the Movement. **63**
        Aquí ¡No!: The Coalition Organizes **66**
    How Material Resources Were Mobilized and Used by the Movement **70**
        Publicity and Information Sharing. **71**
        Demonstrations **73**
        What Is the Impact of the Way Material Resources Are Allocated
        and Used on a Movement's Chances of Success or Failure?. **74**
    Conclusions. **75**

5. Implications for Movements **76**

Bibliography. **80**

About the Authors **86**

Tables and Figures

TABLE 1: Resource Mobilization Matrix Questions **15**

TABLE 2: Material Resources Mobilized by the Three Movements **17**

TABLE 3: Major Funders of the Movements. **21**

**TABLE 4: Cross-Movement Comparison
of Material Resources Mobilization and Impacts** **29**

TABLE 5: Principal Organizations in the Free San Pedro River Movement **37**

TABLE 6: Timeline of the Free San Pedro River Movement		39
TABLE 7: Resource Mobilization Matrix—Free San Pedro River Movement		42
TABLE 8: FASOL Community Dialogue Grants in Nayarit		43
TABLE 9: Principal Organizations in the Movement Against Toxic Mining		53
TABLE 10: Timeline of the Movement Against Toxic Mining		54
TABLE 11: Resource Mobilization Matrix—Movement Against Toxic Mining		57
TABLE 12: Principal Organizations in the Aqui ¡No! Movement		65
TABLE 13: Timeline of the Aqui ¡No! Movement		69
TABLE 14: Resource Mobilization Matrix—Aqui ¡No!		70
FIGURE 1: Chain of Trust		9
FIGURE 2: Virtuous Circle of Resource Mobilization		12
FIGURE 3: Types of Material Resources		18
FIGURE 4: Survey—Kinds of Resources		19
FIGURE 5: Survey—Sources of Resources		20
FIGURE 6: Foundation Funding to the Movements		22
FIGURE 7: Survey—Resources Not Sought or Accepted		23
FIGURE 8: Map of Rio San Pedro River Through Nayarit		35
FIGURE 9: Youth fishing in a village that would be under water following the creation of the dam		46
FIGURE 10: Circle of Resource Mobilization in Nayarit		47
FIGURE 11: January 2011, Tule Beach, SOS Protest		50
FIGURE 12: 40 kayakers spell out "No Mining" on Sept. 2, 2014, outside La Paz		55
FIGURE 13: Circle of Resource Mobilization in BCS/Todos Santos		59
FIGURE 14: Circle of Resource Mobilization in BCS Highway		61
FIGURE 15: Map of Topolobampo, Sinaloa		63
FIGURE 16: "Aquí ¡No!" Campaign Information Flyer		67
FIGURE 17: Demonstration in Topolobampo		68
FIGURE 18: Billboard Showing Consequences of an Ammonia Spill in the Area		72
FIGURE 19: Circle of Resource Mobilization in Sinaloa		74

List of Acronyms

AIDA	Interamerican Association for Environmental Defense (*Asociación Interamericana por la Defensa Ambiental*)
BCS	Lower California South (*Baja California Sur*)
CEMDA	Mexican Environmental Rights Center (*Centro Mexicano de Derecho Ambiental*)
CFE	Federal Electricity Commission
CI	Conservation International
Conagua	National Water Commission (*Comisión Nacional del Agua*)
CRT	Civil Resistance Theory
FASOL	Action in Solidarity Fund (*Fondo Acción Solidaria*)
FRECIUDAV	Citizens' Front in Defense of Water and Life of BCS (*Frente Ciudadano en Defense del Agua y la Vida de BCS*)
GPO	Western Gas and Petrochemicals (*Gas y Petroquímica de Occidente SA de CV*)
ICF	International Community Foundation
IPN CIIDIR	Center for Interdisciplinary Research on Integrated Regional Development
MAPDER	Mexican Movement for People Affected by Dams and in Defense of Rivers (*Movimento Mexicano de Afectados por las Presas y en Defensa de los Ríos*)
MAS	Environment and Society (*Medio Ambiente y Sociedad*)
MIA	Environmental Impact Statement (*Manifestación de Impacto Ambiental*)
NGO	Non-Governmental Organization
PPT	Permanent Peoples' Tribunal
PPT	Political Process Theory
Profepa	Federal Agency for Environmental Protection (*Procuraduría Federación de Protección al Ambiente*)
REMA	Mexican Network of People Affected by Mining (*Red Mexicana de Afectados por la Minerería*)
RMT	Resource Mobilization Theory
SEMARNAT	Ministry of Environment and Natural Resources (*Secretaría de Medio Ambiente y Recursos Naturales*)
SOS	Society Organized for South California (*Sociedad Organizada por Sudcalifornia*)
UAN	Autonomous University of Nayarit (*Universidad Autónoma de Nayarit*)
UDG	University of Guadalajara (*Universidad de Guadalajara*)
UNAM	National Autonomous University of Mexico (*Universidad Nacional Autónoma de México*)
UNESCO	The United Nations Educational, Scientific and Cultural Organization
WWF	World Wildlife Fund

Executive Summary

Nonviolent movements rarely receive funds and have few resources available to them, yet they continue to operate throughout the world, and often bring about fundamental social change. How do they do so much with so little?

This monograph takes three cases of civil resistance movements and analyzes how they mobilized material resources, what it took to do so, and what impacts these materials had on the chances for movement success. We examine three cases from northwest Mexico: the Free San Pedro River Movement in Nayarit (*El Movimiento Río San Pedro Libre*), the Movement against Toxic Mining in Baja California Sur (*No a la Minería Toxica en Baja California Sur* and *Movilización Civil Contra La Minería Baja California Sur*), and the Movement against an Ammonia Plant in Sinaloa (*Aquí ¡No!*). Each of these movements, while regional, is connected to national organizations and movements across the country, such as a national movement of communities affected by dams (MAPDER) or national nongovernmental organizations (NGOs) working with communities affected by mining, such as Mexican Environmental Rights Center (*Centro Mexicano de Derecho Ambiental*). They combine struggles for human rights and the environment, and have carried out a variety of nonviolent civil resistance strategies and tactics over the last decade.

The monograph looks at three types of material resources: goods, labor, and money. For goods, movement leaders mobilized them both in-kind—transportation to demonstrations, t-shirts and bumper stickers bearing symbols of the movement—and in the form of information and research products that supported their cause. Allied NGOs were particularly important in pointing to research that had been done on socioenvironmental issues. In fact, in the case of the dam movement in Nayarit, research conducted by engaged Mexican academics was key to sparking the whole movement.

In terms of labor, the movements successfully turned out thousands of volunteers who gave two forms of support: volunteer and specialist labor. Volunteer labor supported tactics such as nonviolent marches, demonstrations, and appearances at official hearings. Specialist labor brought skills in research, writing, communications, training, theater, facilitation, communications, policy, and environmental and rights issues. All three movements showed great creativity in directing participants' energy, from an offshore demonstration with kayaks that spelled out "No to Mining," to a prominent mural painted on a town wall. Specialists came from universities, national and international NGOs, and from local communities, providing expert scientific analysis of issues from environmental damage to legal representation in court.

Money came in a variety of forms: personal contributions, philanthropic grants, private sector donations, and fishing cooperative dues. For all three movements, money was the hardest resource to come by. Foundation grants were critical to supporting the work of allied NGOs at the national level, but never reached frontline organizations. The one exception was FASOL (*Fondo Acción Solidaria*, Action in Solidarity Fund), which provided small grants to movements at critical moments in their trajectory. The key to FASOL's grants was the use of mentors or advisors who were part of the movements themselves, and thus could direct funds to the right people at the right time.

Crucial to all this work was the persistent strategizing that movement leaders did. Movement leaders constantly assessed their situation and the options open to them, chose strategies and tactics most likely to be successful, and then mobilized resources in support of those tactics. In order to mobilize and strategically use these resources, these movements needed three key capabilities: 1) the ability to unify diverse groups behind a common cause; 2) the ability to effectively strategize and plan operations; and 3) the ability to maintain nonviolent discipline, not giving opponents legitimacy to counter the movements with force. All three movements mobilized a variety of social groups from cooperatives to Indigenous peoples' councils to the general public in support of their activities. They all had committees to generate common messages and coordinate activities, though member organizations, both formal and informal, maintained their independent identities and autonomy. These committees continually strategized about next steps, choosing nonviolent strategies that maximized their impact on opponents at minimal cost to themselves. And despite the fact that nonviolent resistance in Mexico is a dangerous activity, none of the three movements resorted to violent tactics at any point.

With minimal external support, these movements mobilized what they needed when they needed, and took on causes that seemed unwinnable. While none of them achieved all their goals, all of them recorded great victories, and changed the social landscape to ensure that the local people have the organizational capacity, knowledge and resources to help shape their future.

Introduction

Why Are Material Resources Important to Strengthening Civil Resistance Movements?

On a cool, sunny morning in May of 2019, in a coastal town in Mexico, the leaders of the "*Aquí ¡No!*" ("Not Here!") campaign met to discuss next steps against a proposed ammonia plant that threatened fisheries and tourism. Around the table were representatives of some of the local fishing cooperatives, a tourism operator, a former state congressman, a lawyer, a marine biologist and three people from a small non-governmental organization (NGO) who had driven up from the state capital. The authors of this study were invited and present to listen to the discussion of progress, strategy, and tactics for the campaign.

Toward the end of the meeting, a reporter from a local television station came in. As the meeting broke up, the group strategically selected two individuals to talk to her: the young media-savvy tourist operator and the marine biologist. The tourist operator gave great sound bites, and the biologist made the case for why the plant would destroy thousands of livelihoods that depend on a healthy ecosystem. The campaign leaders then indicated that they wanted us to do an interview too. We told them that our Spanish was not good enough for a TV interview, which they laughed off. The reporter switched on the camera and within a day our interview was edited and online.

At that point it dawned on us what was going on. This campaign had no outside support. Yet it had the ammonia company on the run, the majority of public opinion behind it, victories in all court decisions so far, and the support of government research institutions. Where does an all-volunteer movement like this get the resources it needs to function? The answer was in what we saw around the table: skilled pro bono labor from people like the NGO staff and ex-congressman, cash from the fishing co-ops and tourism operators, volunteer efforts from the cooperatives and Indigenous communities, and free publicity from local news outlets. And then what turned out to be a golden opportunity had fallen in their laps: international researchers had come to learn about their work. The campaign leaders at the meeting used our presence to garner more publicity and show that the movement was known internationally, all at absolutely no cost. They acted quickly to connect the resource they had (our presence) to a tactical opportunity to expand their reach with free publicity and the legitimacy of international attention.

Poverty, or the lack of material resources, seems to be so tied to social movements in many people's minds that deprivation and sacrifice—Gandhi's fasts, Mandela's 27 years behind bars writing his autobiography on toilet paper—are *de rigueur* for movement builders. But this cannot be the whole story. Gandhi mobilized not just symbolism on his historic Salt

March but, at the very least, the labor of thousands of volunteers who eventually joined in and walked with him. Movements are certainly not wealthy, but neither do they succeed with no resources at all. They are just very skilled at using what they have or assimilating what they need into their nonviolent tactics.

Having worked with movements for decades, supporting organizations and activists, we seek to understand more about material resources and movements. We have heard (and seen) that the resources a movement mobilizes can create tension among its proponents. We know activists who reflect constantly on the source of funding or the likelihood of agents provocateurs that attempt to embed themselves in the movements by posing as genuine members. We know others who will outright reject almost any offers of assistance that are not from highly trusted sources, or work with people who are not thoroughly vetted and trusted.

This monograph tackles the challenging issue of the role of material resources in the building of effective civil resistance movements. We seek to explain how it is possible for movements to mobilize resources. We hope that uncovering how and where movements have effectively mobilized resources can help both movement leaders and those who want to support them to make more informed choices in deciding what resources to mobilize.

In countries where activism can cause people to be jailed, persecuted, or even killed, the issue of mobilizing resources is a pressing one for movements. We have chosen to focus on Mexico where, despite a dangerous environment (many movement activists are murdered in Mexico each year), activists have managed to build strong civil resistance movements. Mexico also has a long history of movements grappling with fundamental issues of social justice (especially in the fields of rights, environment, gender, and democracy). A good portion of its movement-building takes place under the radar to avoid risks associated with low social trust and high levels of violence against activists.

We wanted to look in a region of Mexico where we have existing knowledge to ask movement leaders themselves about the resources they have mobilized. We focused our inquiry on the Gulf of California area where we have worked for nearly two decades with the Action in Solidarity Fund (*Fondo Acción Solidaria*, FASOL), which supports grassroots social/environmental activists in Mexico. In consultation with FASOL, we chose three current civil resistance movements.

1. **Free San Pedro River Movement in Nayarit:** Citizens across the State of Nayarit came together to oppose the construction of a dam on the San Pedro River that would have inundated land of Indigenous peoples in the highlands, disturbed rich farm and tourist country on the plains, and threatened productive estuaries and the fishing industry on the coast.

2. **Movement Against Toxic Mining in Baja California Sur:** Opposition to the approval of gold mining permits by a largely middle-class coalition stopped the renewal of gold mining in this tourist area.

3. **Movement Against an Ammonia Plant in Sinaloa:** A coalition of fishing co-ops, tourism operators, Indigenous people, environmentalists, and scientists united to block the construction of an ammonia plant that would threaten the livelihoods of thousands and a delicate ecosystem.

Each of these movements, while regional, is connected to national organizations and other movements across the country. They share a struggle of fighting for human rights and the protection of the environment and have carried out a variety of civil resistance strategies and tactics over the last decade.

Informed by discussions with movement leaders, we set out with the idea that movements were able to mobilize material resources most effectively when the resources came from trusted sources within the movements themselves. Our interviews with local activists explored how these movements find and use material resources effectively. In all cases the perspectives of participants complicated any simple understanding of the issue. Indigenous peoples' leaders in Nayarit questioned the very idea of "material resources." In Sinaloa, movement leaders thoughtfully answered our questions but also made us a small part of their "resource story" by using our visit to generate greater publicity. In Baja California Sur, we had very limited access to movement leaders for security reasons and so relied on fewer interviews, more newspaper articles, and previous research on the movement. Given these real-world dynamics that we encountered, we view this study as a preliminary exploration towards the development of a framework for understanding how resources are acquired and deployed and identifying lessons that might be useful to movement leaders, supporters, and researchers.

Material Resource Mobilization in Civil Resistance Studies

The quintessential American community organizer Saul Alinsky wrote in *Rules for Radicals* (1971) that movements are "what you make with what you have." In this monograph, we are interested in how civil resistance movements mobilize the material resources they need. To do so, we must first review how we conceive of civil resistance movements and their broad connections to resources.

Civil resistance movements emerge when people and organizations voluntarily mobilize to systematically withdraw their obedience and strategically apply nonviolent pressure—through a variety of nonviolent tactics such as strikes, boycotts, and mass demonstrations—to disrupt an oppressive system and achieve rights, freedom, and justice (Ackerman and

Merriman, 2014).[1] Véronique Dudouet's observation that "civil resistance is an extra-institutional conflict-waging strategy" (Dudouet, 2017) is useful in understanding that civil resistance, by definition, takes place in an environment where institutional resources, such as courts, legislative committees or regulatory frameworks, do not tend to successfully resolve the issues people are faced with.

These movements unify a wide range of sympathetic individuals, community groups, NGOs, companies, academics and media to build their own power base around movement objectives and goals (Tarrow, 2005; Tilly, 2004; Cohen and Arato, 1992). While this power base is often separate from institutional infrastructure such as courts, legislative bodies or policy-implementing agencies, it is important to note that movements still may try to access and utilize this infrastructure when it is strategically important for them. In the cases reviewed in this monograph, movement leaders themselves added *institutional* tactics to this repertoire, while maintaining a commitment to nonviolent resistance and strategies associated with it.[2]

In recent decades understanding movement resources has become more central in social movement studies. In 1977, Mayer and Zald pointed out that social movements mobilize resources, develop organizing structures, and gain movement allies among the elite (Mayer and Zald, 1977). Rather than being based on social pathology and the free rider problem, as some economic rational choice theorists considered them to be (Olson, 1971), social movements are strategic, powerful, and effective. Resource Mobilization Theory (RMT) has evolved over the years as a way of understanding how movements acquire the resources they need. RMT shares common frameworks with Political Process Theory (PPT), first articulated by Douglas McAdam in *Political Process and the Development of Black Insurgency* (1982). RMT and PPT broadly consider the following elements needed for the success of social movements:

---

1   We add "organizations" to Ackerman and Merriman's definition because organizations enable the consistent discipline and coordination of nonviolent movements in our experience.

2   Movement leaders were very clear that while they employed civil resistance tactics, they also recognized the high potential, in fact the necessity, of engaging in government processes that regulated the dam, mine, and plant—the projects that the movements were challenging. Environmental Impact Statements, government licensing, public hearings, and other public processes stood out for them as the points at which campaigns could intervene to stop or alter the projects. Not only was there high potential for victory, but not engaging these institutional channels would undermine the legitimacy of their complaints in the eyes of the general public. At the same time, leaders recognized that reliance solely on these institutional processes would be insufficient: while these processes are widely seen as legitimate in Mexico, movement leaders also see them as part of a system that is frequently corrupted, or at best acts in favor of corporate interests over those of common citizens. Consequently, movement organizers coordinated civil resistance tactics in tandem with institutional tactics, such as organizing protests and demonstrations to disrupt government hearings and denying permission to enter Indigenous territory to company or government personnel.

1. **Mobilizing structures:** how organizational infrastructure is key to bring people together in common cause, including informal groups, formal NGOs, networks, media, academia, and government allies, and the resources needed to support them

2. **Framing processes:** how an "injustice frame" is developed, showing clearly that there is a problem to be solved (such as lack of civil rights) and proposing alternatives

3. **Political opportunities:** how open a political system is to challenges from outside its elites and social changes that undermine the established political system

4. **Protest cycles:** how resources are available in periods of heightened challenges to elites, often across movements as perception of this vulnerability spreads

5. **Contentious repertoires:** the tactics movements can call on, such as petitions, demonstrations, legal actions, alternative media (Caren, 2007 and Crossman, 2019)

Moving beyond the insights of RMT, Civil Resistance Theory (CRT) researchers such as Ackerman and Merriman (2014) emphasize three internal attributes which this monograph will refer to as strategic capabilities. We believe that these attributes are critical to understanding the capabilities of social movements to assess the need for, effectively acquire, and impactfully deploy specific types of material resources.

1. **Ability to unify people:** how large numbers of people are brought together and unified around movement goals and actions. Movements do this by developing a shared and inclusive vision, and by the presence of legitimate leadership and organizational structure.

2. **Capacity to plan strategically:** how tactics are chosen, and how material resources are developed, deployed and employed to promote the cause to wider audiences.

3. **Nonviolent discipline:** the ability to avoid violent action by movement members, even in response to provocations, increases a movement's ability to attract people and maintain its legitimacy in the public mind (Ackerman and Merriman, 2014; Merriman, 2010).

The insights from both RMT and CRT are largely consistent, although RMT emphasizes the impacts of movement infrastructure and external conditions to a greater extent. Both recognize the necessity to frame an issue in a persuasive way—identifying the problem and the desired solution—and to organize people effectively against opponents. Here we draw attention to the importance of the strategies that movements develop to draw on available resources to give them the greatest chance of success. In this way a movement's strategies focus on finding what is at hand and turning it into resources to support the movement. This entrepreneurial orientation of leaders and members toward resources is key to what they are able to make of them: "social movements depend heavily on political entrepreneurs for their scale, durability and effectiveness" (Tilly 2004).

While RMT makes no explicit commitment to nonviolent discipline, in contrast to CRT, we believe it is implicit in the framework. In general, the theory's "culture of activism" shows little appetite for violent movements. Further, a growing body of evidence from CRT work suggests that nonviolent strategies and tactics are simply more effective at bringing about desired outcomes even against powerful and repressive opponents (Chenoweth and Stephan, 2008 and 2011). These insights of CRT provide further guidance for activists and movement supporters on successful strategies.

Researchers have begun exploring more comprehensively what resources are necessary for the success of movements. Edwards and McCarthy synthesize a useful typology: resources may be moral, cultural, human, socio-organizational, and material. The presence of sympathetic international researchers is a *moral resource*, research produced by academics is a *cultural resource,* skilled labor is a *human resource,* cooperatives and Indigenous people's councils are *socio-organizational resources*, and money is a *material resource*. Each of these categories break down into specific types as well. Moral, for example, may include "legitimacy, solidary support, sympathetic support and celebrity," all of which in turn are mobilized to build the case for the movement and to sustain support for it. Material resources, they note, are "what economists would call financial and physical capital. Including monetary resources, property, office space, equipment, and supplies" (Edwards and McCarthy 2004).

We have found that movement leaders do not, in practice, find these finer categorical distinctions very useful. They deftly consider both non-material resources and material resources without distinguishing them. Leaders make use of what they can mobilize, in whatever form, to craft their tactics. A roadblock, for example, is a viable tactic when they have the organizational and human resources to bring together people *en masse*. They mobilize the material resources needed to mount a roadblock—transport, food, placards—in support of wider movement tactics, and they combine them with other non-material resources, such as getting journalists (human resource) to the protest or organizing the roadblock on a meaningful holiday (cultural or moral resource) to frame the issue.

Even the poorest populations can contribute things that can be transformed by creative application and combination into relevant movement resources. In this way, the more fungible material resources, such as cash and goods (paper, the wall of a building that can become a mural, etc.) may be most helpful in filling in the gaps beyond what movement members already have.

It is the capacity of a movement to strategically determine what resources it will use and when to move forward with its actions and objectives. As Ganz (2005) says, "Strategy is articulated in decisions organizational leaders make as they interact with their environment." This strategy is transformed rapidly with the imperfect knowledge and human intuition of leaders into tactics they believe will result in the changes they seek. Being strategic relies on the ability "to adapt their leadership to changes in their environment and continue interacting with it" (Ganz, 2005). From a CRT point of view, this strategic approach means building decisional and planning capacity, bringing people together under common cause, and mounting campaigns and tactics in a peaceful way. The RMT lens emphasizes the importance of crafting a compelling message, building a movement infrastructure fit for purpose, mobilizing resources to support it, and mounting strategic actions at key times.

The Meaning of Material Resources

In this monograph we focus on material resources, though we think of them not merely as material. In our own work we have found that material resources are infused with cultural and moral meaning for activists in conceiving their strategies. They carry baggage. This point is especially true of money: movement activists who accept money from "tainted sources" can be cut off from the movement for being untrustworthy, or even considered traitors to the struggle. Money can be tainted by being obtained from perceived illegitimate sources such as criminal activity or looted government resources, or from companies and agencies that are complicit in the creation of the problem activists seek to solve.

For material resources, movement leaders are very conscious of who can be trusted to contribute and who cannot, and most are very clear that they will only accept resources from those they trust. The degree of trust varies depending on how far people and groups are from the center of the movement organization—there is no clear boundary between "in" and "out," since there are few rules for entry or exit in a social movement, and the members and opponents tend to be very fluid. Figure 1 illustrates the decreasing levels of trust as one moves out from central movement members and leaders.

FIGURE 1: Chain of Trust

There is a high degree of trust among movement leaders and their organizations, whether formal or informal. Farther along this chain of trust are organizations and individuals sympathetic to the movement, such as university partners or national NGOs. Farther out still are a set of neutral actors that do not take part in the movement itself but provide resources such as studies or general grants. And, of course, at the most distant end of the chain are the opponents. As Tilly (2005) points out, trusted networks are key to managing risk: "When people commit themselves to risky, consequential, long-term enterprises whose outcomes depend significantly on the performance of other persons, they ordinarily embed those enterprises in interpersonal networks whose participants have strong incentives to meet their own commitments and encourage others to meet theirs."

Leaders understand these relationships, and one of their main functions is to manage them: either minimizing the damage from their opposition or incentivizing them to come within the fold. Movement leaders are very conscious of who sits where on this spectrum and will assess the advantages and disadvantages of accepting resources from people depending on where they fall. It is common for movement leaders to disagree on these judgments, which often creates internal conflict within movements.[3]

Philanthropic Support

Money has the distinction of being fungible and relatively easy to direct to a wide array of movement activities. Most movements do not have bank accounts—they rely on participating organizations or individuals to hold and expend funds for them. Philanthropic grants, when they are available, are given to movement organizations, and tend to be designated for purposes that do not overtly challenge elite norms and practices. Groups that express discontent with the prevailing economic system or call for their rights to be protected tend to receive fewer grants (Walker, 2015; Jenkins, 2001). In the current environment of crackdown on civil society activities around the world (the closing space of civil society), philanthropic support for movement organizations that propose innovative solutions which challenge accepted practices is becoming even harder to generate and sustain. As one Indian activist lamented, "There is no space for new answers" (Allan and DuPree, 2018; Carothers and Brechenmacher, 2014).

In Mexico, the philanthropic sector has given little reflection on its own role in providing grants to support civil resistance movement activities, since movement support is outside mainstream philanthropy in Mexico. On the margins, however, some movement-oriented

---

3   Note that an important cultural critique of the concept of resources came from one of the Indigenous people we interviewed. He questioned the Western conception of material resources as separate from the spiritual and social identity of the people, "I have a little problem with the way you speak of resources. To us they are not resources, they are common goods (*bienes comunes*). We in the communities are resisting this way of looking at them as resources" (Movement Interview. Ruiz, Nayarit, Mexico, 26 Apr 2019). Some resources come with a meaning and set of values that can be lost or buried when they are labelled as merely material.

philanthropy appears to be emerging.[4] The collection of material resources continues to be regularly cited in Mexico as important to movement success (Alonso, 2012), but accounts about the capacity of nonviolent movements to raise different types of material resources and the roles these resources play in the accomplishment of movements' objectives are scarce.

Types of Resources and Virtuous Cycle of Resource Mobilization

In order to approach the way that movement leaders think about "resources," we take the framework developed by Toledo and González de Molina (2014), who incorporate resource mobilization centrally into their thinking about social and environmental movements. Movement resources, according to these researchers, are *goods, labor and money*. Others, like Guerra Blanco (2014), identify financial resources, volunteer time, and access to communications resources and the internet as critical resources for movement success.

Note that goods, labor and money include human and even cultural resources that are distinctly not material resources in the Edwards and McCarthy framework. The framework adopted in this monograph also leaves out crucial but intangible resources such as networks, leadership, and grievance or injustice frames. Information and research in this simplified category are cultural resources. Labor can be showing up for a protest (where arguably one's physical presence is very relevant), or the work of professionals and specialists, which is clearly a human resource. In our analysis and empirical investigation, we focus on goods, labor and cash as evidence of an ability to mobilize physical and human capital, and we only address other resources, such as networks or socio-organizational infrastructure insofar as they are intertwined with goods, labor and money for the movement leaders who build their tactics around these resources.

In practice, carrying out a movement tactic is a process in which available resources are used in the service of resistance objectives. Toledo and González de Molina (2014) give a compelling account of this process: organizations or individuals **mobilize** resources, **transform** them into products that are used in support of the movement's tactics, and **apply** them to have an impact. Material resources are thus metabolized into the movement similarly to how living bodies metabolize food, oxygen, and sunlight to enable them to live and thrive.

For example, a school bus may be borrowed (mobilized) to transport protesters to a demonstration. Along the way, it is festooned with temporary signs on its sides (transformed)

---

4   For example, a 2014 partnership between Semillas (a women's movement funder) and FASOL (a socioenvironmental funder) was an attempt to provide greater resources across movements in the country (Barry, 2016). The philanthropic sector has shown some increasing awareness of the need for grants that assist communities. And there are a few studies on the development of civil society that grapple with the scope of volunteer activity, although with little reference to movements (Butcher, 2010; Layton, 2009).

to broadcast the movement's message and then it is employed with its messages and filled with participants as a central part of the demonstration (applied). Figure 2 illustrates this model as a continuous cycle.

Mobilization: The process begins with resource mobilization by which movements figure out what resources are available to them. Leaders strategize about what action would be effective, and what resources they can bring. If institutional processes are not working, movements generate large numbers of people to demonstrate and draw wider attention to the issue. If official studies fail to highlight the problems, then movements find experts to show what is wrong and what alternatives are needed. The tactics leaders choose will dictate what resources are needed.

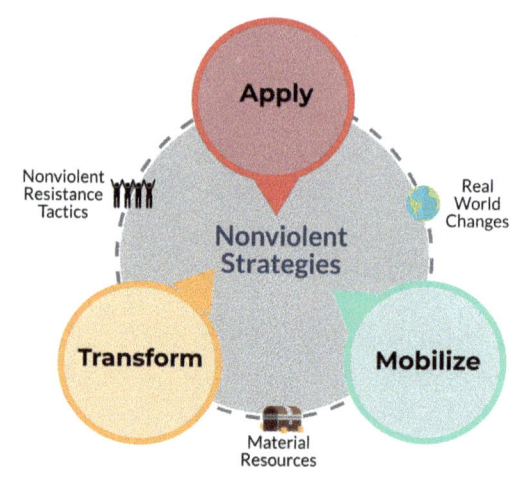

FIGURE 2: Virtuous Circle of Resource Mobilization

In practice, we find that mobilizing resources is a decentralized activity: individuals and organizations are motivated by the messages they hear coming from the movement. These messages are sometimes called "movement frames," an explanation for what the problem is and what the solutions are. This framing of a movement is an argument as to why people should devote their time or money to the cause. These "movement frames" are ideas, stories, etc.—they are not material things. But these stories indicate what money, goods, and labor the movement needs to address the problems. We found that it is rare that a central organization goes out and collects all of a movement's resources. Instead, leaders strategize and organize tactics (like demonstrations or publicity campaigns), and then individuals and organizations generate the people, transport, cash, or whatever resources they can get their hands on to make it happen.

In practice, carrying out a movement tactic is a process in which available resources are used in the service of resistance objectives.

Transformation: Movement participants then transform the resources they have mobilized into forms that are useful for the movement. Examples include turning volunteers into demonstration participants, private cars into group transport, scientists into writers of educational flyers and web content.

This is the *transformation* phase, that is, the stage in which the raw material of resources is transformed into something that contributes to progress. Again, this process relies on the strategic thinking of movement leaders—what is the best use of the people, money, or information that we have at hand? For example, fishermen in boats just offshore are a more powerful symbol for defending fishing rights than the same people in an office somewhere.

The ability to transform a material resource like volunteer time or cash into something useful depends on organizational infrastructure to shape it and to incorporate feedback. It is easier to coordinate activity if there are organizations—whether NGOs, neighborhood groups, or wide networks—since they can strategize and learn from what happens.

Application: Finally, the products of the transformation are applied or deployed with the hope of bringing about social change. Movement leaders take volunteer and specialist labor and apply them to *nonviolent resistance tactics* such as mass protests, participation in public consultations, individual meetings with policy makers, newspaper articles, and public performances. Leaders and members disseminate videos, reports, injunctions, and alternative development projects as transformed movement resources. Volunteer and specialist labor are applied when people understand why they need to act through mass protests, post on social media, provide media coverage, interact with government officials, and promote public dialogue. As more people get involved, their perspectives change the message of the movement itself to accommodate the interests of all groups. When successful, the application of the "products" of transformation results in real world changes, such as increased support for movement goals or even policy change.

Successful application of movement resources also lays the ground for resource mobilization by raising the consciousness of the society to the framed issues at stake, bringing the process full circle.

Nonviolent strategies and the strategic capabilities of movement leaders are at the center of each step of the process. Leaders assess their situation—what is the problem, who are their opponents and possible allies, what resources can they procure, and which are too difficult to find. They develop strategies that minimize the cost to their members and allies while maximizing the costs to their opponents. Since these are often "David vs. Goliath" struggles, the amount of resources does not determine who wins—success goes more often to the side with the best strategies and ability to execute them, including the most effective strategic approaches to deployment of scarce resources to achieve particular objectives.

Successful application of movement resources also lays the ground for resource mobilization by raising the consciousness of the society to the framed issues at stake, bringing the process full circle. A completed "virtuous circle" gives rise to possibilities and a new circle in which goods, labor and money can be mobilized for tactics that take the movement to new levels. Successful events and campaigns generate interest and bring in more people. The success of the application stage thus leads directly to the creation of new resources, snowballing into a stronger movement.

The Monograph's Questions

To explore the relationship between material resources and civil resistance movements, we consider what types of material resources each of the three movements mobilized and used; how they mobilized them; their capabilities to mobilize and use resources; and the impact these resources had on the movements' actions, including their strategies, tactics and eventual outcomes. Our framework is informed by and seeks to answer a series of questions:

1. **How do movements generate material resources?**

    a. How do they mobilize volunteer and specialist labor? What groups mobilize labor? Who provides it?

    b. How do they mobilize other in-kind contributions? What groups mobilize them? Who provides them?

    c. How do they raise funds? What groups raise them? Who provides them?

    d. How do they decide how to make strategic use of their resources?

2. **What capabilities do movements need to be effective at raising, generating, and deploying material resources?** How does the need to mobilize resources affect the movements' ability to choose and sequence tactics during a campaign?

3. **What is the impact of the way material resources are allocated and used on the chances of movement success or failure?**

We combine these three research questions into a matrix table (see Table 1) to provide a schema that we will discuss in each of the three empirical cases of civil resistance movements. Our interviews with activists in these three movements inform this analytical framework. In this way, the table provides a frame to consider the resources mobilized for a given tactic, what capabilities were needed to mobilize and use them, and how these tactics impacted the movement's chances of success or failure itself. It is based on our understanding of how resources are mobilized, transformed, and applied by the three movements. We will return to this matrix in the narrative describing each case, and again in the final analysis comparing all three movements together.

Table 1: Resource Mobilization Matrix Questions

RESOURCES MOBILIZED IN SUPPORT OF KEY MOVEMENT TACTICS[5]	STRATEGIC CAPABILITIES NEEDED[6]	IMPACT ON MOVEMENT CHANCES OF SUCCESS
What types of resources were mobilized for specific nonviolent tactics of the movement?	What capabilities were needed or lacking to mobilize these resources?	What is the impact of the way material resources were allocated and used on the movement's chances of success or failure?

Methods Deployed

We used a mixed methodology, combining 21 semi-structured interviews and five follow-up interviews (in person or over Skype) with 17 movement leaders and four representatives from support organizations, an online survey of 17 movement leaders on their accounts of the use of material resources, and a review of over 200 movement documents and news articles related to the development of the three movements. With FASOL's help, we identified a local movement activist in each case who helped contextualize the issues and open doors with other activists. In addition, we incorporated participant observation, spending three weeks in the region (and have been observers/supporters of these movements for more than a decade) visiting Indigenous peoples' communities, fishing communities and towns in Nayarit, attending movement events in Sinaloa and meeting with the movement spokesperson in Baja California Sur. During this time, we observed working methods, audiences and strategies the movements were employing directly.

Data Limitations and Protecting Privacy

One of the limitations of the data reported in this monograph is that it comes largely from the impressions of the movement leaders. We did not review their organizational budgets or confirm the resources they said they mobilized with the donors and contributors of these resources. In fact, this data is not publicly reported in most cases and the donors do not always link the resources they have given to the movements. We made every effort to interpret the information provided by movement leaders as it was intended. The monograph intentionally does not identify individuals by name outside of where the public record already identifies them because of the extraordinary violence and repression that has become normalized in Mexico today. It also does not attempt to quantify resources in order to protect the privacy of individuals and organizations.

---

5   Following our framework adapted from Toledo, tactics can be widely varied but in this monograph they are assumed to be nonviolent tactics. Resources are grouped into goods, labor and money.

6   Following the Civil Resistance framework, capabilities are broken down into 1) Ability to unify people, 2) Capacity to plan strategically, and 3) Nonviolent discipline.

We prepared this monograph to draw out lessons in a way that can be helpful to campaign organizers in Mexico and other parts of the world. The study also seeks to be useful for funders, support organizations, and policy makers involved in these struggles who are contemplating effective support for other nonviolent campaigns and movements.

1. Comparing the Three Movements

Our review of the three cases allows us to draw some conclusions about the role of material resources in these movements.

How Do Movements Generate Material Resources, and How Do They Decide How to Allocate Their Resources?

Interviews and surveys made it clear that none of the movements separated the task of generating resources from the pursuit of the tactics they supported. No movement had a "resource mobilization" department supporting a "tactics and strategies department," and there was no warehouse somewhere holding resources in waiting for their use. Instead, these three movements strategically planned out their tactics—public protests, communications and publicity, advocacy with government or corporate officials—and then mobilized the resources they needed to make them happen. For example, when movement leaders saw an opportunity for public protest—the SOS gathering in BCS, or disrupting the opening of a highway by the governor in Sinaloa—they then mobilized volunteers to show up, provide transport, and produce publicity items such as flyers and t-shirts. In this sense, movement leaders told us that the two questions of how they mobilized and used resources were intertwined. Their tactics drove the resources they mobilized on an as needed basis.

What Resources Did They Generate?

Based on interviews, document review, and survey results, the three movements mobilized the following resources shown in Table 2:

Table 2: Material Resources Mobilized by the Three Movements

RESOURCE	TYPES	EXAMPLES
Goods	In-kind contributions	Vehicles (cars, buses and boats), gasoline, land, meeting and office space, walls (for murals), chairs, desks, filing space, phones, faxes, computers, paper, posters, food and water, recording equipment (video, photo and sound)
	Information and research	Written reports or research, policy documents, books, internet resources on the issues addressed in the movements
Labor	Volunteer labor	Organizing and participating in tactics such as marches, demonstrations, and appearances at official hearings
	Specialized labor	Both paid and unpaid labor with specialized skills in research, writing, communications, training, theater, facilitation, communications, policy, environmental issues and rights issues
Money		Personal contributions, philanthropic grants, corporate donations, fishing cooperative dues

The empirical data we collected suggests that, as a movement resource, labor is both volunteer and specialist. The difference is that specialist labor, such as the labor of lawyers, artists, engineers, and academics (which can be paid or unpaid), brings specific skills, access to information, or access to the resources of an organization like an NGO or university. In turn, volunteer labor is largely the unpaid participation in movement tactics where skills are less important than the voice and power of citizens acting collectively. For goods, we consider both in-kind contributions—including everything from transportation to paint—and research and information—such as newspaper articles, videos, books, technical studies, and reports.[7] We define money in terms of financing or grants that come from the budgets of foundations or NGOs, and cash contributions from members and volunteers.

This list is summarized in five types of material resources generated by the analyzed movements as presented in Figure 3:

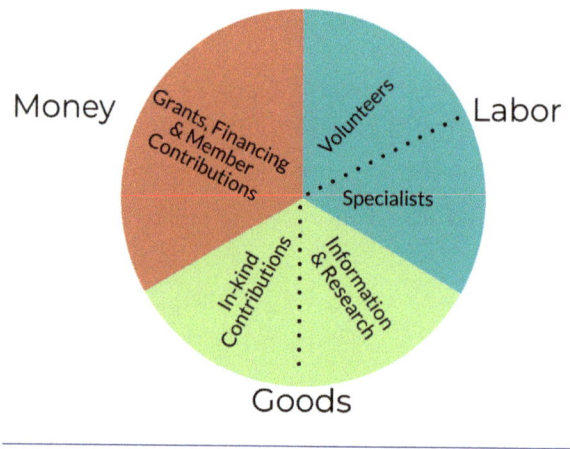

FIGURE 3: Types of Material Resources

Confidential survey results from 17 movement leaders representing all three movements gave a bit more detail for some of these categories. In response to the survey question: "What kinds of resources have you gotten to support your campaign?", movement leaders said the following (See Figure 4). In this survey, movement leaders could select as many types of resources as they had mobilized in their campaigns.

Volunteer labor and meeting space were cited as the most common resources that were acquired and deployed by the analyzed movements (Figure 4). Note that the survey did not

---

[7] Research and information would be classified as "cultural goods" in the Edwards and McCarthy framework. The distinction is a bit fine for most movement activists, who invest a lot of energy in tracking down good information and analysis that they can use to support their cause, so we simplify the concept here to emphasize the existence of a helpful product.

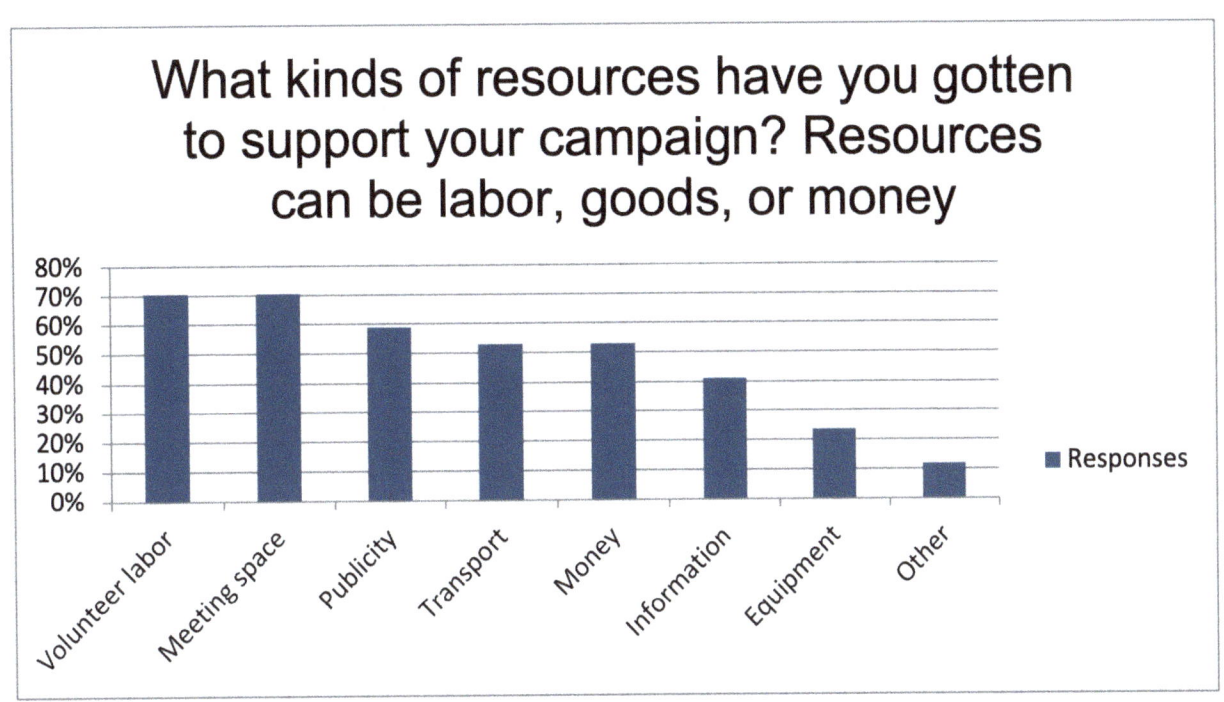

FIGURE 4: Survey—Kinds of Resources

distinguish between unskilled volunteer labor—like showing up for demonstrations—and the more skilled professional labor that interviews and participant observation showed were key in all three cases. No respondents cited grants, research and studies, and physical equipment like computers or office supplies which were provided as potential responses in the survey. Note also that the categories in the survey are phrased slightly differently than the terms used in this monograph, because the data from later interviews and participant observation suggested better terms for these resources that, in turn, informed the case descriptions and analysis. These survey results reflect the provisional language we used at the beginning of the study.

When asked "Which of these resources were most important? Why?", opinions were more mixed. Volunteer labor, including professional expertise, was most cited—"because it gives life to movement activities"—but research and studies and money were also mentioned. Figure 5 shows where movement leaders said they received resources for movement activities:

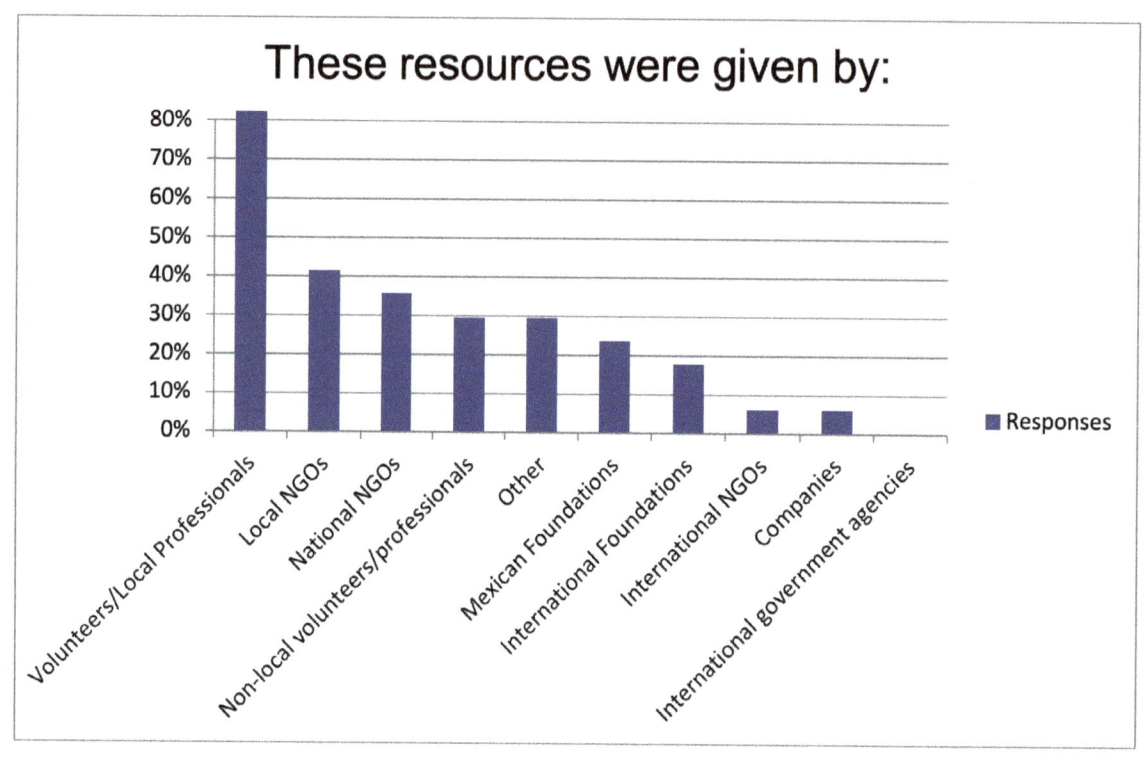

FIGURE 5: Survey—Sources of Resources

Again, volunteers and local professionals were by far the number one source of resources. Local and national NGOs were also important sources. Institutional funding from foundations, companies, and international organizations were least in evidence.

The follow-up question was "Which of these groups gave the most important resources for the success of your campaign?" Many declined to select a single resource, noting that "the resources have been complementary, success has come from counting on all of them." Again, most cited volunteer and professional labor, more than any other category. As for foundations, FASOL was cited by four respondents as the most important, with one citing an unnamed international foundation. Since the three cases were chosen due to their participation in the FASOL program, it is not surprising that it would be mentioned, though it was not clear that it would be cited as one of the most important sources of support.

Larger foundation and government funding were a bit hidden from frontline activists, since the role of this funding in supporting the movements was often behind the scenes. Research on foundation funding for the movements showed that, consistent with the literature, grants went primarily to larger, more established NGOs. Table 3 illustrates some of the grants and support from foundations that we were able to confirm.

Table 3: Major Funders of the Movements

MAJOR INTERNATIONAL FUNDERS	REGRANTING NATIONAL AND LOCAL FOUNDATIONS	NATIONAL NGOS THAT RECEIVED THE FUNDS AND WORKED WITH MOVEMENTS
The David and Lucile Packard Foundation[8]	International Community Foundation (ICF), and Solidarity in Action Fund (FASOL)	Mexican Center for Environmental Rights (CEMDA), and Natural History Society Niparajá
The Ford Foundation[9]	FASOL	
The International Community Foundation (ICF)[10]	FASOL	CEMDA, AIDA
The Charles Stewart Mott Foundation[11]		AIDA
The Global Greengrants Fund[12]	FASOL	

Finally, government funding was also important through the National University of Mexico (UNAM). This funding enabled the Pro-Regiones program to mount public education activities in Nayarit and to do the scientific analysis of the probable impact of the ammonia plant in Sinaloa through the government's Center for Interdisciplinary Research on Integrated Regional Development (IPN CIIDIR).

What did all this money support? It rarely supported frontline organizations, or even directly supported movement activities. Instead, these funds helped pay for program and operational costs for national organizations such as CEMDA and FASOL, which *did* work directly with movement activists, or supported international organizations, like AIDA and WWF, in their work with the campaigns. These groups brought expertise in communications, environmental law, and advocacy in ways beyond what frontline organizations could do on their own. Pro-Regiones provided the information and publicity that sparked the anti-dam movement in Nayarit, and AIDA provided amicus briefs and advice on how to help legal processes succeed. Only FASOL provided funds directly to frontline organizations. Its model of working through a stable group of local activists from all regions of Mexico—"mentors"—enabled it to track movement needs in real time and provide funding on a scale the movements could use when they needed it.

---

8   https://www.packard.org/grants-and-investments/, accessed March 16, 2020. The grants database only covers these years. Actual funding from other years was not available.

9   https://www.fordfoundation.org/work/our-grants/grants-database/grants-all, accessed March 19, 2020.

10 ICF_Grants_List from fiscal year 2014, https://icfdn.org/what-we-do/grantmaking/, accessed March 16, 2020.

11 https://www.mott.org/grants/#s=post_date|desc, accessed March 17, 2020.

12 Global Greengrants Fund, Personal Communication, March 16, 2020.

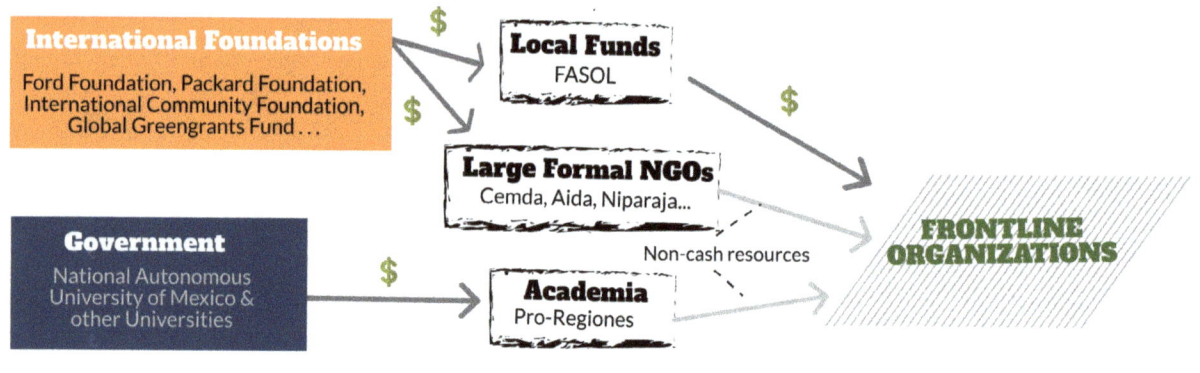

FIGURE 6: Foundation Funding to the Movements

Figure 6 summarizes the flow of funds to these three movements. Larger private foundations, like Ford and Packard, funded NGOs both in the United States and Mexico that then supported smaller groups on the frontline.

The International Community Foundation, Global Greengrants Fund, and FASOL fall into a category of intermediary funders, that is, funders that take large grants from foundations like Ford and Packard and then support local movements using their deep connections and relationships. By the time these funds reached frontline activists themselves—either in cash or in skilled support (non-cash resources)—the source of the funding was often hidden. Only by establishing chains of trust from organization to organization were movement leaders able to make use of these resources.

Given the risk to many movements of disputes over resources, the survey also asked: "Have there been resources that your campaign did not seek or that you refused from...?", followed by the same list of sources.

A third of respondents mentioned that there were companies from which they did not take resources (Figure 7). The reasons varied, but most responded that "the majority do not share our values" or "they would put conditions on the orientation of the movement." The next most cited groups were Mexican foundations, non-local volunteers, and international government agencies. One respondent summed up a general discomfort with resources coming from outside organizations:

> Some resources have been rejected for the simple reason that we do not want to fall into misinterpretations with the people who support us, as it would lend itself to corruption, cooptation, or accusations of being "sold." We accept support only from people

who know or have been integrated into the campaign and we know where they are coming from, and do so in order to really help without receiving any benefit themselves.

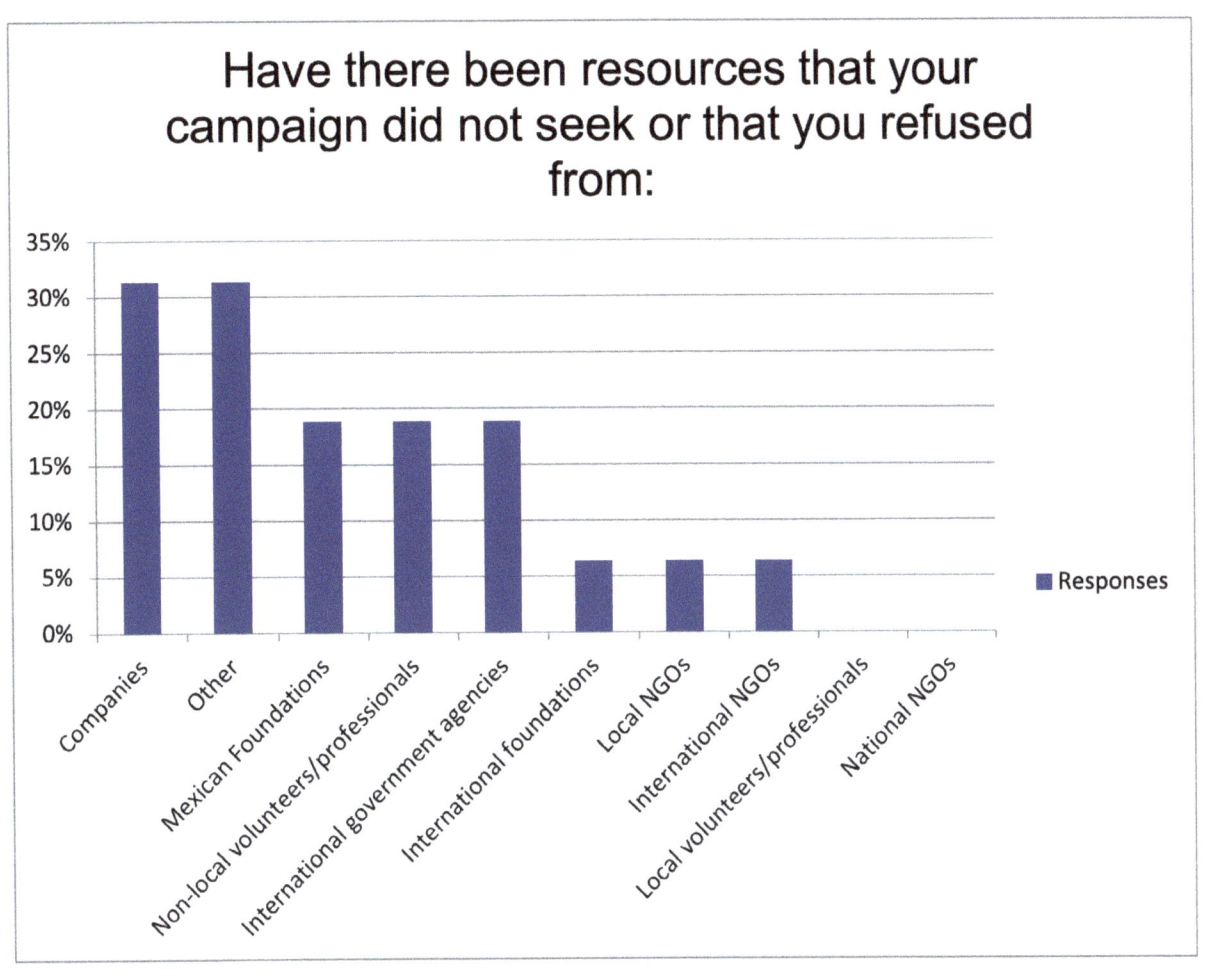

FIGURE 7: Survey—Resources Not Sought or Accepted

Others mentioned the potential damage to the movement in arguments over money "to avoid fragmentation of the group. That almost always happens when there is money," or "Because the resources offered are antagonistic to the objective of the collective. If we accept it, we lose legitimacy." And finally some cited that they simply do not know how to raise money.

One pushback on funding common to many Latin American movements did *not* come up in surveys or discussions. We had expected to find more local resistance to funding from

U.S. foundations than we did, given the proximity and often tense history of American intervention in Mexico. In fact, when activists mentioned U.S. foundations, most told us that their funding was playing a very important role in promoting supportive activities such as research and strengthening larger NGOs.

While all three movements raised the five types of resources—in-kind contributions, information and research, volunteer labor, specialized labor, and money (noted earlier in Table 2)—interviews and participant observation showed that there were both variations and similarities across the three movements around the specific resources they mobilized and how they used them. The relative importance of each resource varied as the tactics changed over time and space. For example, when Pro-Regiones started informing communities of the plans for the dam in Nayarit, there was no movement to speak of. At that point, strategy around disseminating research and information sharing was critical to awaken and mobilize people. Over time, the movement evolved to bring in even more people and to link them in common cause all along the river. At that point generating volunteers willing to organize and spread the word became more important, and in fact transformed the message from the original Pro-Regiones framing of damage to the environment to a focus on the rights of Indigenous peoples and fishermen on the coast.

Likewise, in Sinaloa the most effective resource in the first two years of the campaign was a lawyer that was paid by movement members' generated cash funds and whose legal injunctions on behalf of communities stymied the Ammonia plant in court. Over time, the movement saw that relying only on the courts was risky, since there was no guarantee that the courts would continue to rule on their side, or that government and company officials would not conspire to overturn the rulings, regardless of their legal merits. As a result, the movement then devoted considerable resources to organizing communities and generating volunteers to attend demonstrations, post on social media, and testify in public hearings. These two examples illustrate a common capability of movement success: leaders continuously evaluate outcomes and adapt their strategies as the situation progresses. As their strategies evolve, the material resources that grassroots leaders generate to support movement actions change accordingly.

In general, outside grants were the resource least in evidence, especially for frontline groups, and few leaders devoted much time to searching for them. On the other hand, mobilizing volunteer labor was cited most frequently in all interviews.

It is worth noting that the question of the role of material resources in movement activities stimulated stories about how material resources have fractured or divided the movements, and how movement opponents have used much greater access to these resources to silence movement messages or compromise leaders with pay-offs and bribes. The case of Sinaloa, where movement leaders defected from the movement and abandoned lawsuits thanks to payments from the company, is a clear example of this. Doubts that arose about the commitment of some NGOs to the cause in BCS when they accepted funds from foundations seen as complicit with the gold mining industry is another. Because of this tension, those we interviewed were often very aware of how their own resources were on public display and would be judged. Movement leaders in all three cases said *accountability* and *transparency* of the material resources used for movement activities were concerns.

Were There Any Resources Refused or That Had Negative Consequences?

Activists in all three cases cited resources that potentially could have been very helpful that they did not want to touch. In most cases, these were corporate or foundation donations that had high potential to reduce the legitimacy of activists by coming from "tainted" sources. Tainted sources included the companies that activists were fighting, a *competitor* company whose donations would have undermined movement credibility, or foundations with links too close for comfort to industry.

Beyond tainted sources, some activists were uncomfortable with cash in general, whether personal or institutional, for fear that infighting and accusations of corruption would disrupt the movement. While cash was important at times, activists preferred to accept it from trusted individuals known to them and trusted institutions such as FASOL. Regarding national and international NGOs, the specialists supported by their budgets were crucial to the movement's success. In the spectrum of allies, these NGOs were sympathetic to the movements, though they did not necessarily or explicitly identify themselves with them. Movement leaders did not describe them as being frontline organizations, but their skills and access to grants made them useful allies in the struggle. These bigger NGOs received grants from donors like the Packard Foundation and International Community Foundation, who did not support frontline activists directly. This separation of foundation grants from frontline movement leaders diluted issues of tainted money. Having said that, there were activists who were uncomfortable with some NGOs because of their funding sources.

What Capabilities Do Movements Need to Be Effective at Raising, Generating, and Deploying Material Resources?

We noted above that civil resistance movements need three capacities to be successful:

1. Ability to unify people
2. Capacity to plan strategically
3. Nonviolent discipline

All three of these capacities proved necessary in all the cases for acquiring, mobilizing and using resources effectively.

Unity: In all three cases, the movements started out as independent individuals and organizations with concerns, rather than a unified group of people in agreement on what to do. They were able to join together through strategic organizing that included a wide variety of tactics such as community dialogues, theater performances, and public events such as kayaking. In Nayarit, for example, it took several years of organizing before the disparate interests of the Indigenous peoples upstream defending their territory were brought together effectively with the environmental interests in the towns or the concerns of fishermen on the coast. At that point, the intercommunity council that came together to coordinate efforts was able to craft messages that expressed the concerns of all movement members, and all parts of the movement were able to disseminate messages through their different networks.

The case was similar in Sinaloa. While Indigenous peoples were concerned about their land rights, fishermen cooperatives worried about their livelihoods, and town residents worried about pollution and a decline in tourism. All were able to come together under the *Aquí ¡No!* banner. They each expressed their individual concerns—reporters talking to Congressman Pena heard about biodiversity threats, while those talking to the president of the Twenty-first Century Fishermen's Cooperative heard about shrimp catch rates—but they all shared the communal message of opposition to the ammonia plant.

Key to all three movements was the establishment of a central forum for coordination that provided coherence while activities in the movement remained largely decentralized. Activists in Nayarit created the Intercommunity Council for Sustainable Development of the San Pedro River Basin; activists in Sinaloa came together under the *Aquí ¡No!* Ecological Collective; and activists in BCS unified their movement under FRECIUDAV. These fora improved the capacity of the movements for mutual understanding and planning, though they had limited power over any of the members and different parts of the movement were free to pursue their own interests and tactics. This decentralization was especially important for resource mobilization since different parts of the movements had access to different resources. In the case of Sinaloa, the fishermen's cooperatives had ready access to cash, since members made monthly contributions to the cooperative, and had done so for many years as a matter of course. Restaurant owners in the towns of Los Mochis and Topolobampo had access to cash through their professional association, and access to professional help for graphic design and production of t-shirts, flyers, and banners. Fishermen had their boats and townspeople their cars; both groups mobilized for free to get people to protests. The NGO Bosque a Salvo had access to pro bono professional advice from FASOL in the form of a lawyer who advised groups all over Mexico on their rights and legal options. The *Aquí*

¡No! leadership called on these resources on an as needed basis. All members contributed them directly—nothing passed through the *Aquí ¡No!* Collective.

Strategy: As the movements unified and created these mechanisms of central coordination, they increased their capacity to plan and carry out actions strategically. The interventions of the three movements did not just happen willy-nilly—they were the result of consultation and discussion through the Council, *Aquí ¡No!* Ecological Collective, and FRECIUDAV.

In Sinaloa, the first protest was a spontaneous one, where fishermen challenged the construction workers at the plant site. But as the movement matured and came together, all other protests were planned and timed to create maximum visibility and to make government officials uncomfortable. Holding protests during the visits of the governor and the president not only brought out considerable numbers of people, but also generated news reports and iconic photos that the movement used to draw attention to the issue. This timing not only increased the number of volunteers who showed up, but also the value of their time devoted to the cause. Movement leaders also ensured that there were abundant banners, flyers, t-shirts, and spokespeople visible so that the message of the movement could not be missed.

In BCS, the movement strategically called on its volunteer and professional resources according to the capacities of its members. While the formal NGOs AIDA and CEMDA were not considered "frontline activists," the movement recognized their professional skills in communications and advocacy. These NGOs were able to take messages crafted by the activists and translate them to the national level in the form of a petition and appeals to national officials. In one case, using AIDA's organizational capacity, the movement generated tens of thousands of volunteers to sign a petition, far beyond the capacity of the frontline organizers.

In some ways the strategy and tactics were shaped by what was available to campaigners. While there were small grants from FASOL and contributions by movement members, by and large, cash and grants did not play large roles in any of the campaigns. Instead, movement leaders had volunteers, specialist labor, in-kind contributions, and research and information from other organizations at hand for pursuing their goals. The result was that the movement called on volunteers for public displays of support, specialist labor in communications and legal advice to maximize the value of those volunteers, in-kind transport to get them where they were needed, and the broadcasting of the events widely to draw in wider public support.

It is important to note while all movements made collective strategic decisions, the members then made their own decisions on whether and how to allocate resources. For example, the Council in Nayarit is a central strategy body in the area, but Nuiwari acted independently to support community dialogues. The messages of each participating organization were often tailored to mobilize people in different ways, depending on the audience. In few cases—such as the FASOL grant to the Council in Nayarit—did resources pass through the central coordinating bodies. These coordinating bodies helped make collective decisions, but members then mobilized the resources they had access to and made sure people showed up, banners were there on time, scientists delivered messages, etc.

Larger grants went to the large NGOs—WWF, AIDA, CEMDA—to support their activities and were not available for smaller, local organizations participating in these movements. As a result, movement leaders made use of the research, information, and strategy assistance of these organizations on the dam, mine, and plant for their own tactics. Movement leaders were also supported by AIDA and CEMDA's communications programs, without ever touching money from the big foundations.

Nonviolent discipline: While violence is a fact of life in many Mexican communities—from police, army and private gangs—it was not a major factor in any of the three cases. Despite provocations and dirty tricks by movement opponents, and the disappearance of an activist, movement members and leaders have never resorted to violence, even against property. This fact runs counter to a common myth in Mexico that social movements are often violent. In fact, in all three cases, nonviolent campaigners have continued to make use of state processes for considering big infrastructure projects, speaking at hearings, appealing to legislators and government administrators, and commenting on Environmental Impact Statements. They have done so even in the face of corruption and illogical government approvals. Although, in none of these cases have activists limited themselves to working through formal legal and policymaking processes. In all three cases, such institutional tactics have been accompanied by resistance tactics like protests, blockades, and community organizing.

What Is the Impact of the Way Material Resources Are Allocated and Used on the Movement's Chances of Success or Failure?

As noted above, all three movements acquired, mobilized, allocated and used resources based on the tactics they chose. The tactics were similar in all three cases, though activists called them different things—demonstrations, public communications, community dialogues and organizing, petitions, etc. Table 4 groups these tactics and considers their broad impacts on the movements.

Common Impacts

Table 4 summarizes the most important tactics that the three movements used, and their impacts on the chances of movement success. Here we highlight points where tactics improved these chances and a few instances in which they did not.

Table 4: Cross-Movement Comparison of Material Resources Mobilization and Impacts

RESOURCES MOBILIZED IN SUPPORT OF KEY MOVEMENT TACTICS	IMPACT ON MOVEMENT CHANCES OF SUCCESS
Tactic: Community Dialogues & Organizing Resources Used: • Specialist Labor • Research & Information • Grants & Financing	**Positive Effects** • Established and strengthened cross-community constituencies • Built shared movement frames among diverse communities • Grew public participation and raised awareness **Negative Effects** • Reliance on volunteer labor made it difficult to counter opposition organizing by paid company staff
Tactic: Publicity, Declarations & Petitions Resources Used: • Specialist Labor • Research & Information • Grants & Financing	**Positive Effects** • Raised pressure of citizen demands on municipal, state and national government • Grew movement participation and awareness across many populations but increased opposition among some groups (mining communities in Baja) • Increased volunteer participation and entry of voices of movement leaders in media coverage • Created alternative site of "citizens' policy" to inform policy-making processes **Negative Effects** • Increased risk to individual activists from public exposure
Tactic: Public Marches & Demonstrations Resources Used: • Volunteer Labor • Specialist Labor • Cash & In-kind Contributions	**Positive Effects** • Enabled movements to demonstrate wide public support • Shared identification with the resistance movement across communities • Increased support of local government and made state government "pay attention" • Grew public participation and raised awareness
Tactic: Use of Institutional Government Processes Resources Used: • Volunteer Labor • Specialist Labor • Research & Information	**Positive Effects** • Exposed the issue and promoted public accountability of municipal, state and national officials and agencies, eventually forcing them to take positions • Allowed passive allies (business and associations) to identify with the movement • Mobilized power of courts • Tied up opposition in court and with additional research requirements **Negative Effects** • Early success with legal challenges may have delayed grassroots organizing in Sinaloa
Tactic: Blockade of Roads & Occupation of Airports (Baja) Resources Used: • Volunteer Labor • Cash & In-kind Contributions	**Positive Effects** • Display of power energized core activists • Influenced government officials, including state governor and the new president

Community Dialogues and Organizing

In all three cases, organizing community members against the projects being proposed was key to building a mass-based and coherent movement. As a result, movement leaders invested in community meetings, networking with existing community-based organizations and Indigenous governing bodies, and the use of social media to get their messages out cheaply. They also brought in staff from national and international NGOs and universities to provide expert advice on the projects, and used their research materials in crafting messages. The result for the movements was growth of public support, recruitment of more volunteers and specialist labor (both paid and unpaid), the transition to more visible civil resistance tactics, and the creation of central coordinating bodies. The growth, diversification of tactics, and unification all contributed to the power of the movements. If the movements had relied simply on expert testimony and studies, without organizing community opposition, it is unlikely that they would have successfully blocked the mine, dam, or plant.

The downside of relying on community organizing is that the movements had difficulty competing against their opponents' paid staff with considerable budgets. Movements relied primarily on volunteers, while opponents were able to utilize paid staff, vehicles, and consultants to counter their efforts.

Publicity, Declarations, and Petitions

In all cases, communities were faced with large, complicated infrastructure projects. Before any opposition could begin, movement leaders had to reframe the discussion from the rosy benefits put out by project promoters to the costs and damage that would result as well. To do so, all three movements sought access to research and information (especially on technical and scientific issues), specialist labor in both technical areas and in communications, and volunteer time for movement members to disseminate this information broadly.

The larger NGOs and universities with their specialist staff were key to getting this information and reformulating it as an alternative view to those of their opponents. The impact of these alternative messages was to create unity of messaging within the movements, and to broaden public support in general. It was important in all three cases that there was a central coordinating body that generated these messages, bringing in all perspectives, not just those of environmental specialists or Indigenous leaders. As a result, this method allowed different communities to emphasize what was important to them while staying unified behind the central messaging. This central coordination prevented the splintering of the movements.

The contrast to this point is that when the movements did not take into account all perspectives, communities opposed them. The clearest case was in BCS, where the movement was never able to accommodate the perspectives of working miners, whose livelihoods were threatened by the opposition to mining.

Public Marches and Demonstrations

All three movements at times chose to bring people out into the streets (and the water) to raise the visibility of the movement and make things uncomfortable for authorities. The formats ranged from the symbolism of physical bodies spelling out "SOS" in BCS to the disruption of photo opportunities for politicians in Sinaloa. This tactic is the clearest demonstration of the value of volunteer labor, though hidden in these demonstrations is the donation of in-kind transport, meeting space for planning, specialist labor for graphic design or event planning, and sometimes cash for production of educational materials or banners.

The impact on the movements was increased public support for their causes and greater access to decision makers with increased evidence that their messages were being heard, such as when activists got their messages to the president of Mexico in both Sinaloa and BCS.

Use of Institutional Government Processes

As large projects with social and environmental consequences, all three projects were required by Mexican law to conduct environmental impact studies, hold public hearings and consultations, and obtain government approvals, especially in Indigenous territory. Movement leaders recognized these moments in the formal processes as points of vulnerability for their opponents.[13] Not only was approval at each stage not guaranteed, but these events also drew attention from the press and media and created an opportunity to disseminate messages more widely. This was especially clear in the case of BCS, as movement mobilization around these events exposed and prevented backroom deals, forcing government officials to be accountable. Again, volunteer and specialist labor were important here, as were research and information on open-pit mining, water and the environment that were produced by the national and international NGOs involved, especially CEMDA and AIDA. This case highlights that while most civil resistance tactics were deployed by the frontline organizations, support in institutional processes by NGOs which employed paid professionals using donor money, often from abroad, was a critical complement to local community organizing. Without the demonstrations and publicity generated by communities, it is unlikely that a few NGOs could have stopped these projects. The converse is also probable—without the support of technical information and professional communications, it is unlikely that local communities could have prevailed on their own.

---

13   In the language of Resource Mobilization Theory, Mexico provides "political opportunities" for movements to make real change through government systems. This stands in contrast to some other countries where the level of repression or corruption is so high that institutional mechanisms are not likely paths to success.

All three movements used the courts at different points in their trajectories. The Sinaloa case showed that overreliance on the use of courts left the movement exposed to setbacks in the court. Even worse, when the movement prevailed in court, it found that the company was able to go behind its back and induce community leaders to renounce their lawsuits, undermining the whole process. In this case, reinvigorating its community organizing and education and its protest tactics proved crucial to defending fragile gains in court.

Blockade of Roads and Occupation of Airports

Only the Baja California movement escalated public resistance to the level of a blockade. The resources necessary to block a highway, and then two airports, went far beyond the usual demand for volunteers, since they needed to remain in place until the state relented. The tactic was ultimately successful as the governor announced he would not support the mining project, though it came with a high risk of a violent response from the police.

2. The Free San Pedro River Movement, Nayarit

Overview of the Movement

In 2007, Mexico's Federal Electricity Commission (CFE) was moving forward on the Las Cruces dam project[14] on the San Pedro River, the seventh largest river in Mexico, to provide electricity and water resources for regional development. CFE claimed the project would affect few people (El Universal, 2008), but research suggested that the dam would dry up vast stretches of wetlands, damage biodiversity, threaten farming and fishing, and inundate land considered sacred by Indigenous peoples' communities (Dominguez Serrano, 2013).

Few people along the river had any idea of what was coming or had any input into the plans. After learning about the plans in a series of intensive community dialogues, residents began the Free San Pedro River Movement (*El Movimiento Río San Pedro Libre*), a civil resistance movement to protect the river that has stalled but not yet permanently retired the Las Cruces project. Over the twelve years from 2007 to 2019, the movement grew to encompass a diverse coalition of Indigenous peoples' communities, fishing cooperatives, and residents of towns along the river with support from national and international organizations in Mexico.

The Seed of the Movement

As the planning for Las Cruces was underway in 2008, Pro-Regiones, a project at the National Autonomous University of Mexico (UNAM) to improve regional development strategies by linking universities, brought together academics and representatives from the World Wildlife Fund (WWF) and Conservation International at the Autonomous University of Nayarit (UAN) to discuss the case of the potential damage caused by the project. They proposed a strategy to enable what they called "critical social analysis" to engage affected communities in the legal/political processes related to the project and collect better data about its potential impacts (Rodriguez, 2015).

After the meeting, Pro-Regiones began an extensive awareness-building campaign aimed at conducting community dialogues across the entire river basin region. Several NGOs got involved including Nuiwari and EcoJusticia Nayarit (EcoJustice Nayarit), both of which work in the state on sustainable development issues, the Interamerican Association for

---

14 The US$795 million plan has roots in the Northwest Hydraulic Plan (PLHINO), along with the Hydraulic Plan for the Northwest Gulf (PLHIGON) formulated in the 1970s, which considered large infrastructural investment to be the most effective path to regional development. The plan, which dates back more than 80 years, has already resulted in the construction of two major dams in the state (Aguamilpa and El Cajon) with a third La Yesca under construction (Dominguez Serrano, 2013).

Environmental Defense (AIDA), the Mexican Center for Environmental Rights (CEMDA), and the Mexican Movement of People Affected by Dams and in Defense of Rivers (MAPDER).

Growing Resistance Through Dialogue

The official narrative on Las Cruces suggested that it would have very limited impacts and only on a small number of people in the Highlands. The awareness-building campaign enabled NGO leaders and researchers to hold community dialogues with an aim of countering this narrative by both building solidarity up and down the river and constructing an alternative narrative on the impacts of the dam informed by research and local knowledge. Movement leaders in Nayarit described these dialogues as critical for resisting the official narrative.[15] For example, an Indigenous woman leader in the movement says she first found out about the dangers of the La Cruces dam in 2008 when,

> Someone came from outside. I don't know where. He knew what was going on and what was going to happen. Some of us said we do not want the dam. We thought about how we get water in our houses, for our families, plants and animals. When we thought about how it will be more difficult to have pure water, we became united.[16]

A movement leader from the fishing cooperatives says he first met with Pro-Regiones at an Earth Day fair in 2009 held at the University of Nayarit in Tepic.

> I felt our livelihood was at immediate risk. We rely on the flow of the water into the mangroves. We talked to them about organizing and there was born the movement.[17]

The dialogues sparked resistance in communities in the three distinct regions through which the river wends. The highlands, where Las Cruces would inundate some 5000 hectares, is the home and sacred territory[18] of Cora (Nayeri), Tepehuan and Wixárika (Huichol) Indigenous peoples (Del Castillo, 2011; Moreno, 2015).

---

15 Ackerman and Merriman note that "building and maintaining unity is multifaceted, but the foremost aspect of doing so is developing a shared and inclusive vision for a civil resistance movement" (2014, p. 6).

16 Movement Interview. San Juan Corapan, Nayarit, Mexico, 27 May 2019.

17 Movement Interview. Boca de Camuchin, Nayarit, Mexico, 28 Apr 2019.

18 The Muxatena in the San Pedro River basin, a rock formation, is considered a sacred site by the Nayeri. There, they celebrate Saint John's Day every June 24, with flowers, traditional dress, music and dance. The Muxatena is also visited by Huicholes, Tepehuanos and Mexicanos (Méndez, 2014).

FIGURE 8: Map of Rio San Pedro River Through Nayarit

Midway in its path, the river passes through the town of Tuxpan and a flat landscape that depends on it for farming livestock, beans, sorghum, tobacco, bananas, and mangoes, as well as for the domestic and international tourism it draws (Figure 8). On the coast, fishing communities ply the rich estuary which is fed by the San Pedro where it empties into the Gulf of California. The estuary serves essential ecological functions in supporting a thriving fishing industry in the area. This area includes a biosphere reserve (*Reserva de la Biosfera Marismas Nacionales*), federally constituted in 2010 with 20 percent of Mexico's mangroves and robust biodiversity.[19] Fishing communities in the area are familiar with destroyed fisheries up and down the coast due to poor river management.

These different regions were threatened in different ways by the dam. They had little experience in working together in a common struggle. Both the coastal fishers and the Indigenous peoples' communities, however, have long histories of struggling against state or elite repression. Opposition to the dam brought the three regions together in common cause, thanks to the strategic work of NGOs, Pro-Regiones staff, and Indigenous and grass-roots leaders.

---

19   33 varieties of reptiles, eight amphibians, 52 mammals, 188 birds and 60 fish.

The Pro-Regiones strategy resulted in over 200 meetings and actions to publicize information about the Las Cruces project and its potential impacts.[20] "This was a first step in bringing order and sense to the [movement's] activities."[21] Pro-Regiones, Nuiwari and EcoJusticia are three organizations that convened many of these activities, but the movement began to draw on participation from more than two dozen local, national and international civil society organizations (some organizations mentioned in interviews are included in Table 5).

On July 9, 2009, an intercommunity council (*Consejo Intercomunitario para el Desarrollo Sustentable de la Cuenca del Río San Pedro*, the Intercommunity Council for Sustainable Development of the San Pedro River Basin—shortened here to the Council) launched to support the growing resistance and fight for the sustainable development of the San Pedro River. The Council expressed the central concerns of the communities along the river in a declaration shortly thereafter which garnered more than 5,000 signatures between July of 2009 and January of 2013. It made seven points of opposition:

1. the river is not a commodity that can be sold;

2. the hydroelectric project does not constitute a sustainable development option;

3. the jobs that would be created would be precarious and provisional, the energy generated would not be clean or intended to meet the needs of the region, and the intended flood control would be inappropriate;

4. taking water from this region to promote development in other places, compromising local possibilities, would be inadmissible;

5. the exclusion suffered by the inhabitants of the basin in this project is socially and politically unfair;

6. the most predictable scenario would be the dispossession of land and resources and a severe environmental crisis with negative productive, social and cultural impacts; and

7. the "organized, coordinated and peaceful action of all the inhabitants of the region, will allow… the government and the Nayarit society to be called upon to fully assume this great discussion and abide by its results" (Rodriguez et al, 2015).

---

20   These actions include radio appearances, information meetings and assemblies, conferences, round tables with specialists in ejidos (a local community government unit in Mexico), cooperatives, rural production associations and Indigenous communities with support of UNAM, WWF, FASOL and the Packard Foundation (Rodriguez et al, 2015).

21   Movement Interview. Tuxpan, Nayarit, Mexico. 27 Apr 2019.

Table 5: Principal Organizations in the Free San Pedro River Movement

TYPE OF ORGANIZATION	ACRONYM	NAME
PRINCIPAL ORGANIZATIONS IN THE MOVEMENT		
ENVIRONMENTAL RESEARCH AND ACTION		
Domestic NGO	CEMDA	Mexican Environmental Rights Center (*Centro Mexicano de Derecho Ambiental*)
Domestic NGO	Pro-Regiones	Pro-Regiones
Domestic NGO	SuMar	SuMar for Nature (*SuMar por la Natureza*)
Domestic NGO	Manglar	Mangrove Ecological Group (*Grupo Ecológico el Manglar, A.C.*)
Domestic NGO		Ecojustice Nayarit (*Ecojusticia Nayarit*)
Domestic NGO	Nuiwari	*Nuiwari, A.C.*
International NGO	AIDA	Interamerican Association for Environmental Defense (*Asociación Interamericana por la Defensa Ambiental*)
International NGO	PPT	Permanent Peoples' Tribunal
Network	MAPDER	Mexican Movement for People Affected by Dams and in Defense of Rivers (*Movimento Mexicano de Afectados por las Presas y en Defensa de los Rios*)
University	UAN	Autonomous University of Nayarit (*Universidad Autónoma de Nayarit*)
University	UNAM	National Autonomous University of Mexico (*Universidad Nacional Autónoma de México*)
University	UDG	University of Guadalajara (*Universidad de Guadalajara*)
CONSERVATION		
International NGO	CI	Conservation International
International NGO	WWF	World Wildlife Fund
INDIGENOUS PEOPLES' RIGHTS		
Indigenous Network		The Intercomunity Indigenous Council (*El Consejo Intercomunitario Indígena*)
Indigenous Governance		Indigenous Nayeri Council (*Consejo Nayeri*)
Indigenous Governance		Indigenous Wixárika Council (*Consejo Regional Wixárika*)
FUNDING		
Domestic Foundation	FASOL	Action in Solidarity Fund (*Fondo Acción Solidaria*)
International Foundation	Packard	David and Lucile Packard Foundation
COMMUNITY ORGANIZING		
Network		Intercommunity Council for the Sustainable Development of the San Pedro River (*Consejo Intercomunitario para el Desarrollo Sustentable de la Cuenca del Río San Pedro*)

Organizing gathered steam in 2009 as CFE was busy preparing an Environmental Impact Statement (*Manifestación de Impacto Ambiental*, MIA) as required by law to be submitted to the Ministry of Environment and Natural Resources (*Secretaría de Medio Ambiente y Recursos Naturales*, SEMARNAT). Table 5 shows the organizations that have come together in the movement.

National organizations telegraphed the concerns of the movement to a national audience. AIDA, in alliance with SuMar, Nuiwari, the Council, CEMDA and the Council Nayeri, created the website *Defiende Muxatena*[22] which provides information on the movement's campaigns. With the Council acting as a host, the Mexican Movement of People Affected by Dams and in Defense of Rivers (MAPDER) held its national meeting in Los Reyes, Nayarit, from October 5 to 7, 2012, to draw attention to the struggle for the San Pedro.

Those with whom we spoke told us of a number of public demonstrations. One person counted at least two large demonstrations with as many as 5,000 people and three smaller protests in Tuxpan, Tepic, and even far away in Guadalajara in the neighboring Jalisco state. The protest in Tuxpan on September 9, 2012, brought together over 2,000 people carrying signs and marching through the streets to demonstrate their solidarity against the dam). Resistance also took the form of discouraging researchers from entering the territories to do fieldwork for the MIA. Those we interviewed, however, believe these researchers ignored their warnings and came anyway.[23]

Despite this resistance, CFE submitted the MIA to the General Directorate of Environmental Impact and Risk of the Ministry of the Environment and Natural Resources (SEMARNAT) in December of 2013. Having failed to deter the submission, the movement then focused on demanding for SEMARNAT to reject the MIA, since CFE could not go forward without it.

At this point Mexican law required the company to hold public meetings with Indigenous communities to get their consent. Community members packed into these meetings to express their opposition.[24] A flurry of local and national press quoted movement leaders, focusing especially on the opposition of Indigenous leaders. In the ten months between December of 2013 and September of 2014, at least 13 articles were written about the opposition to the dam. AIDA also launched a website, *Defiende Muxatena,* to fuel the public campaign in this period. More protests were held in Tuxpan, Tepic, and Guadalajara.

The tension in the region was high in September of 2014, when SEMARNAT announced that it was authorizing the MIA, giving CFE the permission it needed to move forward (Somselmedia, 2019). In the central plaza of San Pedro Ixcatan, a crowd of around 500 heard the CFE research team cite a total of 33 consultations with Indigenous peoples' representatives. It explained (again) that the dam was essential to expand electricity production to meet

---

22 **https://defiendemuxatena.wordpress.com/**.

23 Movement Interviews: Boca de Camuchin, Nayarit, Mexico, 28 Apr 2019, and San Juan Corapan, Nayarit, Mexico, 27 May 2019.

24 In Rosarito, officials arrived "without announcement" to get the community to sign a call for an extraordinary general assembly that would give consent for the expropriation of its land (Méndez 2014).

increased energy demand in the future.[25] Participants learned as well that SEMARNAT was attaching conditions. One of these was for CFE to produce a social impact assessment in compliance with Mexico's Electricity Industry Law.[26] As of the time of writing this assessment has not been carried out.

Reaction to the news came quickly. More than 50 academics and 80 organizations delivered a petition in the next two weeks to Mexican President Enrique Peña Nieto, demanding that he and the head of SEMARNAT, Juan Jose Guerra Abud, revoke the authorization of the Las Cruces project (Mendez, 2014). The Indigenous peoples' councils for the Nayeri and the Wixárika (*Consejo Indigena Nayeri* and *Consejo Regional Wixárika*) collaborated together on a joint statement in December condemning the dam and accusing the government of violating their rights (Cordero, 2014). Table 6 shows a timeline of movement-related activities.

Table 6: Timeline of the Free San Pedro River Movement

TIMELINE OF THE FREE SAN PEDRO RIVER MOVEMENT		
2008		ProRegiones Meeting at UAN
	23 Oct	1st CFE, UDG, UAN agreement to conduct environmental impact study
2009	19 Jul	Intercommunity council (Consejo Intercomunitario para el Desarrollo Sustentable de la Cuenca del Río San Pedro) established
	4 Nov	2nd CFE, UDG, UAN for environmental impact study
2010	12 May	Reserva de la Biosfera de las Marismas Nacionales created
	By Dec	> 200 community dialogues took place with various specialists and CSOs
2012	April	Incorporation of the Comite de Comunidades Nayeri, strategic alliance with the Consejo Wixaricka
	Oct 6/7	IX Encuentro Nacional del Mapder in Presido de los Reyes – "All voices: free rivers!"
	January	Declaration reached more than 5000 signatures
	Sep 9	Public demonstration of about 2000 people in the city of Tuxpan
2013	Dec 9	CFE submitted Environmental Impact Statement to SEMARNAT
	Feb 20	Public information meeting. San Pedro Ixcatan
2014	Jan 19	Anti-dam cultural march and demonstration in Tepic
	Sep 28	SEMARNAT authorized Environmental Impact Statement for Las Cruces Dam
2017	May 23	The Wixarika filed a request for protection against SEMARNAT, Conagua and CFE
	May 28	Wixárikas y Náyeris met in Rosarita to launch the Keiyatsita Declaration
2018	April	AIDA presented Amicus brief in support of Wixarika request for protection
2019	February	Diverse groups asked president to retire the Las Cruces project

In mid-2017, members of the Wixárika filed a request for an injunction (*amparo*) against CFE and the national water agency (*Conagua*) arguing the dam project was a violation of their rights. They stressed Mexico's need to comply with international treaties and the

---

25 In San Pedro Ixcatan, representatives of CFE and state government showed up with armed guards on Dec 15 to make a request for the community to allow CFE to carry out technical studies around land use changes and compensation (Del Castillo, 2013).

26 Condition I required CFE to comply with Article 20 of the Electricity Industry Law to present a social impact assessment providing an assessment of social impacts and its plans to mitigate them.

irreparable damage the dam would inflict on their cultural, social and economic well-being. In the same week, the Wixárika and Nayeris launched the Keiyatsita Declaration, which acknowledged the responsibility of both peoples as guardians of sacred places. The next year, AIDA supported the Wixárika request for protection by submitting an amicus, or "friend of the court" brief, noting that the dam would be in contravention to six international treaties[27] to which Mexico is a party (SinEmbargo, 2018).

It is not clear that the political will has hardened sufficiently against the dam project to secure its cancellation. By 2019, there has been no resolution to the Wixárika request for protection. Over 80 civil society groups have called on the new president to permanently retire the Las Cruces project supported by a study by SuMar concluding the dam is simply not financially or strategically viable (Gonzales Lefft, 2019). SuMar's director, Ernesto Bolado Martínez, is quoted as saying, "Investment in renewable technologies on a small scale and near the place of consumption is more attractive for investors, more strategic for the national electricity system and more efficient for distribution networks." However, the project has not been removed from consideration as the new government is seeking ways to generate clean electric power and meet the needs of consumers.[28]

Organizing communities from 2009 to 2019 has resulted in hundreds of meetings up and down the river. While the campaign has not succeeded to get the Las Cruces project permanently canceled, many movement leaders believe it has succeeded in raising the stakes for the dam to go forward.

> For us it was triumph that the dam is not being constructed. Thanks to our work we have shown with numbers and studies that it is not feasible. They [CFE] know why we don't want it. Our movement is a unique battle for social justice in Nayarit, defending our resources. The second success is that we forced a new study [the social impact analysis required by SEMARNAT] and were able to mobilize academics from the university.[29]

How Material Resources Were Mobilized and Used by the Movement

What material resources—goods, labor and money—did the movement mobilize for its activities? What capabilities did it need to mobilize them? And when did the resources help or hinder the movement? Movement leaders assessed what resources were available to them and what power they had in the face of government control and the ever-present risk of

---

27 For example, Convention 169 of the International Labor Organization requires free, prior and informed consent of communities that will be affected by large scale development projects.

28 A recent article rumors that work is about to begin on the foundations of the dam (Aguilar, 2019).

29 Movement Interview. Tuxpan, Nayarit, Mexico, 27 Apr 2019.

violence against them. From this assessment they developed a variety of nonviolent strategies and tactics. We identified four tactical areas of resistance activities in the twelve-year struggle:

1. community dialogues;
2. publicity, declarations and petitions;
3. exerting alternative authority; and
4. public marches and demonstrations.

This list is not meant to be exhaustive. It is drawn from 11 interviews, visits to both upstream and downstream communities, and a review of over 50 news articles and publicly available movement documents.

Movement leaders also mentioned other civil resistance tactics such as withholding permission for CFE representatives and researchers associated with the Las Cruces project to visit community territory around the river during its preparation of the Environmental Impact Statement (MIA) and afterwards. Interviews suggested four communities refused to give permission to CFE staff in San Juan Ixcatan to investigate land use changes and payments to affected communities. Since we were unable to find sufficient information on how this permission was denied, we are not including it in the list of tactics discussed.

Table 7 summarizes what resources were mobilized and what they were used for. The second column notes what movement capabilities were needed to effectively use these resources. The third column summarizes the impact of this use of resources on the chances of movement success. As we laid out in the introduction, resources are goods, labor and money. Capabilities are organized by the categories of the Civil Resistance framework: 1) Ability to unify people, 2) Capacity to plan strategically, and 3) Nonviolent discipline.

Table 7: Resource Mobilization Matrix—Free San Pedro River Movement

RESOURCES MOBILIZED IN SUPPORT OF KEY MOVEMENT TACTICS	STRATEGIC CAPABILITIES NEEDED	IMPACT ON MOVEMENT CHANCES OF SUCCESS
Tactic: Community Dialogues 1. <u>Specialist Labor</u> Academics & NGOs connected with Pro-Regiones 2. <u>Research & Information</u> Impact of dams in general and potential impacts in Nayarit as brought by academics & NGOs 3. <u>Grants & Financing</u> University & NGO budgets & 8 small grants from FASOL	**Unity** Those who participated in the Pro-Regiones meeting had a shared analysis that dam project posed a threat to communities on the river. **Strategy** Pro-Regiones meeting conceived a focused information and dialogue campaign as shared strategy of participating groups.	Creation of an intercommunity constituency along the river as a civil resistance movement.
Tactic: Publicity, Declarations & Petitions 1. <u>Specialist Labor</u> Communications and legal staff from collaborating organizations 2. <u>Research & Information</u> Videos, communications equipment & information on the potential impacts of dams 3. <u>Grants & Financing</u> NGO budgets & 2 small grants from FASOL	**Unity** Council's ability to craft a unified message for national & local groups with intersecting objectives. Some divergence of objectives with WWF. **Strategy** Council's elucidation of a civil resistance strategy against the dam project.	Increased volunteer participation and entry of voices of community leaders in media coverage. Raised awareness on national level of struggle.
Tactic: Public Marches & Demonstrations 1. <u>Volunteer Labor</u> More than 5000 volunteers 2. <u>Specialist Labor</u> Staff & representatives from collaborating organizations 3. <u>Cash & In-kind Contributions</u> Demonstration space, placards, banners, transport & food contributed by volunteers or by collaborating organizations	**Unity** Coordination & implementation capacity by Council & collaborating organizations to mobilize volunteers from highland, plains and coastal communities. **Nonviolent Discipline** No evidence of violence in any of the public demonstrations.	Shared identification with the resistance movement across highlands, plains and coastal communities. Increased support of local government and made state government "pay attention."

The movement made use of all five types of material resources identified in the monograph introduction (see Table 2): Volunteer Labor, Specialist Labor (including skills and knowledge), Cash & In-Kind Contributions, Research & Information, and Grants & Financing. These resources were mobilized after the strategy and plans for resistance tactics became clear. In each instance, movement leaders focused on these tactics and not on the material resources that were required for them. The following sections elaborate on the findings summarized in Table 7 to draw observations on resistance tactics from interviews with movement leaders. It considers how and why material resources were transformed into movement goods and applied to tactics, and what this meant for the success of movement campaigns and objectives.

Community Dialogues

The community dialogues shaped the Free San Pedro River Movement. It may never have emerged, at least at the time it did, without them. The dialogues took the form of over 200 activities to inform and stimulate conversations in communities—from community meetings to one-on-one discussions at regional events like the Earth Day celebration to radio interviews. The dialogues resisted the state's power to frame the Las Cruces project as benign. Interviews highlighted the importance of specialist labor, research and information, and grants and financing to the dialogues.

Academics and NGO staff (**specialist labor**) from the Pro-Regiones project at UNAM, Nuiwari, EcoJusticia, and Manglar who knew about the potential impacts of the dam provided critical guidance and information to the dialogues. These academics and NGO staff provided and interpreted information from reports and studies (**research and information**). Financing for the specialist labor and some project costs came from the institutional budgets of the participating groups: Pro-Regiones, Nuiwari, EcoJusticia and Manglar. Movement leaders said they were unaware of many grants raised directly for this work, however, they believed support from the David and Lucile Packard Foundation and the World Wildlife Fund to these NGOs for their environmental work in general was important. FASOL also provided eight small grants for more direct support of movement activities (see Table 8), facilitated by a "mentor." FASOL mentors are volunteers who are familiar with the work of the community groups and bring them to FASOL for grants. They also monitor and mentor grantees as they implement the projects.

As for the capabilities needed to mobilize and make use of these resources, the small core of participants in the Pro-Regiones meeting created sufficient **unity** around the analysis of the problem—that affected communities were unaware of the potential threats of the Las Cruces project both to their own communities and for their neighbors up and down the

Table 8: FASOL Community Dialogue Grants in Nayarit

COMMUNITY DIALOGUES – GRANTS FROM FASOL (2010–2013)		
YEAR	ORGANIZATION	PROJECT
2010	Nuiwari A.C.	Las Cruces information & awareness-building campaign
2010	Delegation of groups	Participation of Nayarit groups in the MAPDER meeting "Rivers for Life"
2011	Nuiwari A.C.	Las Cruces information and awareness-building campaign in Nayeri and Wirárika communities
2011	Community committees from San Pedro Ixcatan and San Juan Corapan	Exchange of experiences among dam-affected communities to strengthen and improve grassroots strategies
2011	Intercommunity Council for the Sustainable Development of the San Pedro River Basin	Dissemination of information on the Las Cruces Project
2011	Indigenous Committee for the Defense of the People	Meeting of Indigenous communities for the organization of the original people
2011	Pro-Regiones	Social environmental study in the basin of the San Pedro-Mezquital River
2013	Community of Dialogue and Knowledge	Environmental awareness building in the Presidio of Los Reyes, in the municipality of Ruiz, Nayarit

river—to mobilize academics and NGO staff from UAN, UNAM, Nuiwari, EcoJusticia and Manglar. This shared analysis of the issue helped to focus their **strategy** on nonviolent, community dialogues to get relevant information to communities in a form they could understand and act on. To carry out these dialogues, they used their existing organizational budgets and professional staff, paid by the university and donors to the NGOs. A FASOL mentor (who identifies grants for the organization) was mentioned as key in all interviews in bringing some direct support for movement activities. The mentor developed a focused strategy to support building linkages among the river communities through interconnected grants.

The key **impact** of the specialist labor, research & information, and grant financing was the creation of an active, informed constituency from the highlands to the coastal areas of the San Pedro River that became a nonviolent civil resistance movement. All the movement leaders with whom we spoke cited these dialogues as critical to the formulation of this resistance. The inclusion of active dialogues also framed the movement narrative as specific social, economic, environmental and cultural impacts as understood by the communities and expressed in the first document the Council produced in 2010. The access to specialist labor (the mentor) and small grants from FASOL that supported the community dialogues were cited by many movement leaders as motivating factors, although they believed the dialogues would have happened anyway, though less rapidly and effectively.

Publicity, Declarations, and Petitions

Once communities began to resist the imposition of the Las Cruces dam, they found themselves with plenty of volunteers but without the resources to formulate and pursue a publicity campaign.

> We lacked things (information, primarily) to write to inform people. We had no loudspeakers, no access to radio and tv. What we had was volunteers. Small amounts of money came out of our pockets. We also had no access to the internet and no presence on the internet.[30]

Publicity campaigns relied largely on press interviews given by members connected to the Council and supplemented with the communications efforts of collaborating NGOs and networks (AIDA, CEMDA, EcoJusticia, Manglar, MAPDER, Nuiwari and SuMar).

As the community dialogues progressed from 2009 to 2011, the **specialist labor** of academics and NGOs was joined by new voices of community leaders from up and down the river expressing resistance against the Las Cruces project. Twenty communities (including Rosamorada, Ruiz, El Nayar, Acaponeta, Tuxpan, and Santiago) from upstream down to the

---

30   Movement Interview. Tuxpan, Nayarit, Mexico, 27 Apr 2019.

coast expressed opposition to the project at meetings held with CFE and other authorities in their communities.

The Council, AIDA, and CEMDA also began to mobilize media (**using volunteer and specialist labor**, and **research and information**) by getting radio appearances and interviews with journalists, reflected in more than 120 articles and 300 videos uploaded on YouTube between 2009 and 2019.[31] Movement members told us that social media was useful for gaining support outside the state. There is a Facebook page,[32] the *Defiende Muxatena* website,[33] and a number of YouTube videos.[34] National and regional organizations—AIDA, CEMDA, MAPDER and SuMar—widely publicized the struggle in their own organizational communications activities.

Monetary support (**financing and grants**) for communications activities came from the participating NGOs using their own budgets (raised as part of their general fundraising, not for this movement in particular). The Council, AIDA and CEMDA made the movement part of their communications programs. We do not know the extent to which other organizations such as EcoJusticia, Nuiwari, and Sumar or the Indigenous councils and fishing cooperatives also made communications part of their organizational efforts, but all are mentioned in various news articles and videos produced about the Las Cruces resistance. The Council and the Intercommunity Indigenous Council each mobilized about US$4000 in grant funding from FASOL in 2012 for their work in hosting the IX MAPDER meeting that helped them to disseminate information and prepare for coordination and facilitation of the meeting.

In terms of **capabilities**, the establishment of the Council was key for its members to craft **unified** opposition messages, making it possible for collaborating organizations (EcoJusticia, Manglar, Nuiwari, Pro-Regiones and the local Indigenous councils and fishing cooperative) to mobilize volunteer labor with a consistent message. The communications advocacy capabilities brought by communications staff from AIDA and CEMDA enabled delivery of movement petitions and communications directly to government offices or national press that resulted in press coverage. Some divergence in the objectives around the movement reduced the clarity of its message but it is unclear if this had any effect on the ability to mobilize volunteers or media. Many movement leaders mentioned that they believed WWF was driven by

---

31   A google search in July of 2019 produces 126 news articles and 315 uploaded videos on the impacts of CFE's Las Cruces project in Nayarit.

32   Rio San Pedro Mezquital Libre at **https://www.facebook.com/riosanpedro.mezquitallibre**

33   **https://defiendemuxatena.wordpress.com/**

34   Examples: **https://www.youtube.com/watch?v=IqOkW1vY6aQ** or **https://www.youtube.com/watch?v=5CtjmvAEufw**

FIGURE 9: Youth fishing in a village that would be under water following the creation of the dam.

environmental objectives that did not take into account the non-environmental impacts of dams on the river communities (Rodriguez et al, 2015; various interviews). The existence of a coordinating council enhanced movement **strategy** by coordinating messages by a representative body.

One of the key **impacts** of these resources was that media inclusion of local activist voices from the Council raised the movement's local credibility and increased volunteer participation. As one Nayeri movement leader said, "The most effective resources for us have come from NGOs and from the media—the radio. [Having this press coverage] made us realize that we were not alone."[35] The inclusion of AIDA and CEMDA helped the movement respond on a national level with *Defiende Muxatena* and actions such as the 2014 petition against the dam delivered to the president and head of SEMARNAT.

Public Marches and Demonstrations

Protests escalated leading up to and after CFE released its Environmental Impact Statement (MIA) in December of 2013. As Figure 10 illustrates, the ability to craft unified messages and strategies enabled movement leaders to transform civic space, specialist labor and volunteers into a series of protests. Nobody we interviewed seemed to know the exact number of demonstrations, but they estimated between four to six public protests were held in 2013 and 2014.

Media inclusion of local activist voices from the Council raised the movement's local credibility and increased volunteer participation.

In this period, public marches against the dam were held in Tuxpan and Tepic (the capital of Nayarit). The protest in Tuxpan in September of 2013 brought together hundreds of people and closed off several streets. Figure 10 illustrates how movement leaders organized the September 2014 Tuxpan demonstration by mobilizing information, people, civic space, materials, and transportation, transforming them into messages, volunteers and specialist labor, and a protest space. The application became a well-organized protest that increased visibility

---

35 Movement Interview: Presidio de Reyes, Nayarit, Mexico, 27 Apr 2019.

for the movement in local and state government and their ability to mobilize even more volunteers.

It is not possible to give an estimate of the **volunteer labor** involved in these demonstrations since there are no authoritative reports of the number of participants or demonstrations, but a rough figure based on estimates from Tuxpan and Tepic suggests they involved more than 9,000 people and 70,000 volunteer hours. The **volunteer labor** of the members of the Council was key to the organization and dissemination of the dates, times and objectives of the demonstrations.

In terms of **in-kind contributions**, the coastal communities, movement leaders said, contributed buses, but most participants found their own transportation across the significant distances to the demonstrations by private cars or vans. The permission to use public roads and squares for protest activities was also important. In the Tuxpan protest, the municipality gave organizers the space and a permit, according to one movement leader.[36]

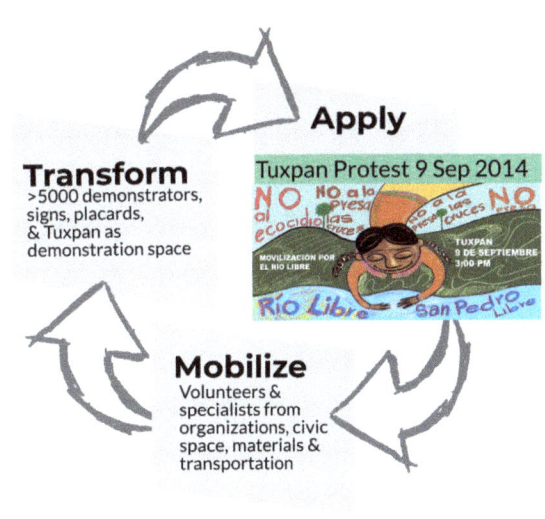

FIGURE 10: Circle of Resource Mobilization in Nayarit

Fishing communities and Indigenous peoples largely led the resistance. But the Council also **unified** those communities with residents of the towns who were more motivated by environmental concerns than by Indigenous rights or protecting fisheries. The ability of the Council to unify these different groups enabled protests and demonstrations. The unity of environmentalists in the towns also contributed to the movement's ability to mobilize protest space and support from city officials. The public demonstrations with organizations from up and down the river maintained **nonviolent discipline**, with no reported incidents of violence.

Movement leaders mentioned that key **impacts** of the thousands of volunteers who participated in public demonstrations were the strengthened commitment of communities to

---

36   He also said the Nayarit state government was asked to provide permission for the assemblies but refused (several interviewees suggested that the governor of the time was benefitting from the dam project). By 2016, Governor Roberto Sandoval is quoted as saying in reference to Las Cruces, "...some political actors have complicated the great projects that Nayarit has to move forward." He pledged to visit CFE to ensure that development is not halted, despite the dam having been removed from its slate of priority projects at that time because of budgetary constraints (Carvajal 2020).

a shared cause across the highlands, plains and coastal areas and the increased visibility with the government. The protests provided an opportunity beyond the smaller dialogues for communities to share the struggle for the river, "And the government paid attention. The marches were critical points in building the visibility for the movement."[37] One movement leader said the ability to work together and learn from each other had not only strengthened his organization's activities but that it had benefitted him with ideas for new projects and economic activities.[38]

In another way, although the protests alone were not successful in forcing CFE and SEMARNAT to cancel the dams, they may have led to the greater use of legal tactics as a strategy to fight the dam through the mobilization of Indigenous peoples' communities. Movement leaders said that use of the courts as institutional means to supplement the non-violent civil resistance strategies was a relatively new strategy for Indigenous peoples' groups, who are skeptical of these institutions. In mid-2017 members of the Wixárika submitted a request for protection (*amparo*) alleging that the Las Cruces project violated their right to self-determination, autonomy, territory and cultural identity.[39] The next year AIDA supported the request for protection by submitting its own amicus brief to the federal courts. Interviews with movement leaders stressed that legal assistance (supported by AIDA, EcoJusticia and grants from FASOL) has been a very important resource to help them understand the legal arguments against the dam's violation of the constitutions and international treaties. Civil resistance tactics largely subsided with the use of the courts, but the links and solidarity built over the resistance period are continuing across the river communities that say they remain vigilant in looking for signs that the Las Cruces project will be reinitiated.

Conclusions

The Free San Pedro River Movement has not yet succeeded in winning conclusive protections for the river, but it has had important outcomes. The mobilization of volunteers from all along the river has built a strong movement core and linked the highlands, plains and coastal communities that had little understanding of each other. And even within these areas, it has built capacity for different groups to work together. This is especially interesting among the

---

37   Movement Interview. Tuxpan, Nayarit, Mexico, 27 Apr 2019.

38   Movement Interview. Presidio de Reyes, Nayarit, Mexico, 27 Apr 2019.

39   "...since a 188-meter curtain is planned to be built within their sacred territory in the San Pedro River basin that will impact more than 4500 hectares, and will completely and irreversibly modify the hydrography, the morphology, the sediments and minerals, and the fauna and flora of their ancestral territory that they access to carry out their cultural and spiritual traditions" (CEMDA, 2017).

Indigenous groups who are often fractured and yet, through their work in the movement, were able to craft the joint statement of the Wixárika and Nayeri peoples.

It may also be a very interesting model for academic and NGO leaders to replicate elsewhere, where they can create the conditions for an authentic movement by providing the information and convening space that not only informs but also gives people linkages with each other and the tools needed to formulate their own resistance.

Very few grants and in-kind resources were mobilized overall in the movement, but both individuals and organizations were able to draw from their own resources for their resistance activities. We did not detect that this use of the individual and organizational resources created significant tradeoffs. In fact, one Indigenous leader told us that he did not think of his investment of time and transport over the last decade as a contribution to the movement because it has enabled him to be more effective in his community bringing projects and ideas that he would otherwise never have known about.

3. Movement Against Toxic Mining, Baja California Sur

Overview of the Movement

In January of 2011, more than 8500 people showed up on Tule Beach between Cabo San Lucas and San Jose del Cabo on the southern tip of the Baja Peninsula to demonstrate their opposition to the proposed *Los Cardones* mine that would bring open-pit gold mining to the state of Baja California Sur (BCS). They arranged their bodies into the shape of the letters S.O.S. (see Figure 11) to send a call for help in stopping the proposed concession that was steam-rolling through political back channels and that they believed would endanger the region's natural resources and precarious water situation. The letters also stand for *Sociedad Organizada por Sudcalifornia* (Society Organized for Southern California), one of more than ten local organizations who had helped to mobilize the demonstration.

FIGURE 11: January 2011, Tule Beach, SOS Protest

Photo provided by NO A LA MINERÍA TÓXICA EN BAJA CALIFORNIA SUR, MÉXICO Facebook Group.

Over the next eight years, the movement would grow to encompass dozens of organizations across the state and become a significant force against the *Los Cardones* mine and against the mining industry's intentions to exploit the state's mineral wealth.

Gold Mining in the State

Gold and silver were first discovered in BCS in 1862 but this initial gold rush all but ended by 1926. *El Triunfo*, one of the main mining communities in the mountains (the Sierra de la Laguna mountain range cuts through the southern center of the peninsula), for example, was once in line to be the capital of the state (Robinson, 2019). Today it has shrunk from a population of more than 10,000 to under 300 people. Now tourism and agriculture largely fuel the economy, with a population swollen by transplants from other states seeking a more laid-back lifestyle and relative affluence. BCS also has robust communities of ex-patriates from the United States and Canada who purchase or rent vacation homes.

However, BCS still has plenty of gold. Efforts to resuscitate the industry date back at least to the 1970s when Echo Bay in Canada began exploration, and then in the 1990s sought permits for its proposed *Paredones Amarillos* open-pit gold mine. Because of the significant environmental impacts, its request for permits had not been successful. It subsequently sold its interest in the mine to Vista Gold Corps, which reorganized the proposed mine under the name the Concordia Project (*Proyecto Concordio*), and tried to get permits that were again denied in 2010. The mine was again renamed *Los Cardones,* and Vista Corps sold 60 percent of its ownership in the mine to Invecture Group and the Zapal Development company (*Desarrollo Zapal*), its local subsidiary linked to Billionaire Ricardo Salinas Pliego, owner of the Aztec TV group. Forbes lists Pliego as the 122nd richest man in the world with an estimated net worth of US$12.8 billion (Forbes, 2019). The *Los Cardones* gold mining project, while the center of resistance, is not the only mining interest in BCS.

The Consolidation of Resistance

Playing an important role in the early resistance, *Agua Vale Más que Oro* (Water is Worth more than Gold) was launched in 2009 by professionals from the tourism industry (Ibarra Mesa, 2019). They saw *Los Cardones* as a direct threat to tourism, because of its potential impacts on both environmental attractions and water supplies, crucial for the tourist towns on the Cape and La Paz. In addition to ocean attractions, the Sierra de la Laguna Biosphere Reserve was set up in 1994 and has since been designated a Global Biosphere Reserve by UNESCO. A 2015 expedition in the Biosphere identified 877 species, 29 of which are on the endangered species list and 107 that are found nowhere else in the world (Pskowski, 2016).

From 2009 to 2019, over 50 organizations[40] have been involved in the movement, and many thousands of people have actively participated in its resistance activities. While we have been working in the state for many years, we were not able to speak with many of these organizations because of an agreement to maintain confidentiality for those who have participated in movement activities. Half of these organizations are small, community-based organizations that are located in both the rural and urban areas of the state. Another quarter are professional, business and academic associations, and the last quarter are national or international organizations, some of which, such as CEMDA (The Center for Environmental Rights), maintain offices in the state.

This concern for confidentiality arises from the clear threats associated with speaking out against private interests. Violence is always a possibility—across the country, there were over 30,000 murders in 2017 alone (Turak, 2019), some of those targeting activists and

---

40   This is a count of organizations identified in interviews, movement documents and newspaper articles.

politicians. Many activists report facing harassment and threats (SDPNoticias, 2015). This violence was a major motivator in sticking to nonviolent strategies and tactics.[41]

Movement's Strategies to Expose Wrongdoing

Since the local permits had already been issued in secret for *Los Cardones*, one of the primary strategies for stopping the gold mine was to convince the national environmental ministry, SEMARNAT, to turn down the Environmental Impact Statement. But this was difficult to do, given a history in which the company repeatedly changed hands and its ability to mobilize its powerful connections to some of the most influential corporate and government organizations in the county. Since opposing corruption is an issue that motivates large numbers of Mexican citizens, movement leaders realized it was thus critical to expose the deals in order to hold local agencies accountable for allowing the mine to go forward. Following this strategy, leaders sought to get not only large numbers of people to local government meetings but also the right people, including representatives of important social and economic interests in the state.

It seemed that every time the movement made headway the company was able to change strategies to reinvigorate the project. Many activists believed that the state government was on their side, but in 2015, in the final days of its administration, the Urban Ecology and Energy Secretariat suddenly approved the company's land use change request for the mine (Pskowski, 2016) without the consent or even the knowledge of many citizens. Challenging perceived corruption in Mexico often gets you killed, so movement leaders realized that sustenance of nonviolent actions and strength in numbers were essential. The members of this movement were largely middle class, with significant stake in the growing economy of the state. They needed the protection of numbers to make it extremely hard to target specific individuals and organizations.

A dense network of NGOs and community-based organizations worked together in the Movement against Toxic Mining in the region over the last decade (Mejia en la Paz, 2010). Table 9 shows the scope and type of organizations that were involved. FRECIUDAV (the *Frente Ciudadano en Defense del Agua y la Vida de BCS*, or the Citizens' Front in Defense of Water and Life) became the main coordinating body of this network. It helps to coordinate civil resistance, communications and policy activities of the movement. It claims more than 30 collaborating organizations but does not release the names or contact information of the individuals it coordinates.

---

41 One illustrative example of the dangers of organizing is the case of David Sosa Perez, who was the spokesperson for SOS. He disappeared in October 2011, leaving a wife and children behind, after speaking out against the mine. He has not been seen since (Olson, 2011). There are no details or clues as to his fate, or whether or not his disappearance was related to his work on the campaign.

Table 9: Principal Organizations in the Movement Against Toxic Mining

PRINCIPAL ORGANIZATIONS IN THE MOVEMENT		
TYPE OF ORGANIZATION	ACRONYM	NAME
FUNDING		
Domestic Foundation	FASOL	Action in Solidarity Fund (*Fondo Acción Solidaria*)
International Foundation	ICF	International Community Foundation
International Foundation	Packard	David and Lucile Packard Foundation
ENVIRONMENTAL RESEARCH AND ACTION		
International NGO	AIDA	Interamerican Association for Environmental Defense (*Asociación Interamericana por la Defensa Ambiental*)
Domestic NGO	CEMDA	Mexican Environmental Rights Center (*Centro Mexicano de Derecho Ambiental*)
International NGO		Mining Watch Canada
Domestic Network	REMA	Mexican Network of People Affected by Mining (*Red Mexicana de Afectados por la Minereria*)
Domestic NGO		Water is Worth More than Gold (*Agua Vale más que el Oro*)
Network (Campaign Coordination)	FRECIUDAV	*Frente Ciudadano en Defense del Agua y la Vida de BCS* Citizen's Front in Defense of Water and Life of BCS (*Frente Ciudadano en Defense del Agua y la Vida de BCS*)
Domestic NGO	MAS	Environment and Society (*Medio Ambiente y Sociedad*)
Domestic NGO	Niparajá	Natural History Society Niparajá (*Sociedad de Historia Natural Niparajá*)
Domestic NGO	SOS	Society Organized for South California (*Sociedad Organizada por Sudcalifornia*)

With the exception of FRECIUDAV, opposition to *Los Cardones* or mining in general in the peninsula is not a primary activity of any of these groups, although it often fits with the mission of the environmental NGOs and CBOs in the region. Because opposition to mining is risky, civil resistance activities appear to have been largely conducted as performances that highlight the central messages about the dangers of toxic mining without highlighting individuals. Important fact sheets often reveal no authorship. They are disseminated as seemingly decentralized public opposition at public meetings. They are also found on websites and a robust Facebook page[42] in which the movement has largely the appearance of a many-headed hydra.

Apex of Civil Resistance

Opposition to the mining project appears to predate the 2011 protests, although in this study we have focused on the campaigns and activities after that time. Table 10 gives a timeline of key activities.

---

42 No to Mega Mining (No a la Mineria Mega), see **https://www.facebook.com/NoMegaMinasBCS**.

By far the most intense period was in 2014 and 2015. For 37 days in April and May of 2014, over 300 protesters camped out at the steps of the governor's palace and the La Paz municipal offices (municipalities are legal divisions in Mexico roughly equivalent to counties) to demand the revocation of gold mining concessions the municipality had recently granted in addition to 33 other mining concessions (Ibarra Mesa, 2019).

In September of 2014, 40 kayakers spelled out "No Mining" in a demonstration in front of the city of La Paz (Figure 12). Also that month, 2,500 residents of Todos Santos (population around 6,000) lined up to sign the Todos Santos Pact, which consists of eight points in opposition to the installation of mining megaprojects in this region (BCS Noticias, 2014). The Pact's declarations begin with, "We oppose, and will oppose with all the necessary actions, both legal, as well as through disobedience and peaceful civil resistance, the installation of mining megaprojects in this region, since we do not accept that death sentence signed by SEMARNAT." It continues to call on all popular representatives to oppose the mine and connects the movement in La Paz to a national movement against transnational and national corporate predators that violate the constitution, human rights and treaties signed by Mexico (Pact of Todos Santos, 2014).

Table 10: Timeline of the Movement Against Toxic Mining

TIMELINE OF THE MOVEMENT AGAINST TOXIC MINING		
1978/ 2009		Echo Bay (Canada) opened 150 ha gold mining project in BCS as Paredones Amarillos. Project was rejected by SEMARNAT & state government twice, the 2nd time as Proyecto Concordia.
2009		First call to action of civil society in Todos Santos and Pescadero. Water is Worth More than Gold. Environment and Society established.
2011		Vista Gold sold to Invecture Group and its subsidiary Desarrollo Zapal S.A. of C.V. Permits reactivated.
	March/ October	SOS's David Sosa Perez published complaint in La Jornada. He disappears on October 24.
2012		CEMDA and Niparaja engaged.
	Feb 15	Vista Gold sold 60% of its shares to Invecture Group through Desarrollo Zapal.
2014	Jan 9	SEMARNAT public meeting responding to citizen pressure.
	April/May	300+ demonstrated for 37 days at Government Palace and the Municipal Palace of La Paz. City Council and Mayor signed pledge to give no mining permits.
	Sept 2	Kayakers demonstration in La Paz against mining.
	Sept 12	The Pact of Todos Santos.
	August	SEMARNAT received negative opinion from the Protected Areas Commission.
2015	August	Public information meeting held in La Paz. 60 representatives of groups oppose.
	Sept 23 – Sept 26	100+ residents of Todos Santos blocked Transpeninsular Highway at Pescadero. Over three days, protestors occupy airports in Cabo & La Paz. Government of BCS rejects mining agreement of La Paz.
2018	March	Federal judge in Mexico City ordered recognition of land use changes.
2019	March	President announced cancellation of Los Cardones project at launch of water desalinization plant in Cabo San Jose.

When the state government still refused to hear their concerns, they escalated civil resistance by creating a blockade at Pescadero just south of Todos Santos that closed the main artery to Cabo San Lucas and, as events escalated, by occupying the airports in La Paz and Los Cabos, the main route for all goods and tourists, until the Secretary of State agreed to meet with them (BCS Noticias, 2015). The state under this pressure from local residents finally rejected permit requests for the *Los Cardones* mine. However, much of the uncertainty revolves around the La Paz municipality's grant of land use change for the mining area (La Jornada, 2016).

Intervention by the Courts

A series of court rulings in August and September of 2018 ruled for the *Los Cardones* mine, seeking to force the La Paz municipality to honor its original sign-off on the mine (Medina, 2018). But the La Paz council, in no small measure due to the activism and mobilization of the local population, refused to honor the permits it said were issued secretly. Following suit, in 2017, the movement submitted its own request for protection (*amparo*) calling for the environmental ministry to cancel permits granted for *Los Cardones*. As of March 2020, the court had not ruled on the injunction.

FIGURE 12: 40 kayakers spell out "No Mining" on Sept. 2, 2014, outside La Paz.

Francisco García

But while waiting for the results of the judicial action, activists showed up to ask newly elected President Andreas Manuel Lopes Obrador (the first in over 80 years to not hail from the ruling Institutional Ruling Party, PRI) for his position on the mine on his first visit to the state after the 2018 elections in January of 2019. Despite having expressed clear reservations around mining as a candidate, Obrador appeared to be taken off guard and equivocated, saying he would need to get more information. This position changed significantly by early March when he came out publicly against the issuance of mining permits in BCS. He announced at the inauguration of a desalinization plant in Cabo San Lucas, "We have to take care of paradise, not destroy paradise, take care of nature. And if I'm talking about people living on tourism, we have to take care of the environment. And if I'm talking about water supply, we have to take care of the water in the subsoil." (Baja Post, 2019).

In 2019, the Federal Courts ruled decisively against the *Los Cardones* mining project because protected areas legislation in the country requires potential extractive projects to prove residency in an area. The judge ruled that the company lied on its application. With the current political will against the mine in the region and the protection afforded by the biosphere, it now looks unlikely that *Los Cardones* or similar mining initiatives can succeed there. But movement activists continue to be skeptical in a country where mega-wealth often finds a way to subvert legal restrictions.

How Material Resources Were Mobilized and Used by the Movement

This section considers the role of material resources in building the movement: how they were used, what they were, the capabilities of movement that made them useful or not, and the impact that they had on the movement itself. Movement leaders assessed what resources were available to them, and what strategies and tactics might be effective. In this case we focus on tactical areas of resistance activities.

The struggle against Los Cardones and its earlier iterations has evolved into a movement against "toxic mining" in BCS, engaging over 40 organizations and thousands of citizens for nearly a decade.

The struggle against *Los Cardones* and its earlier iterations has evolved into a movement against "toxic mining" in BCS, engaging over 40 organizations and thousands of citizens for nearly a decade. The movement has mobilized significant material resources largely from self-financed volunteers who participate in demonstrations and official public information meetings, produce a variety of communications materials like artwork and social media postings, and, most recently, support legal action. Links to the local business community, academia and government bureaucracy are also strong, where, at the very least, many of the movement leaders are employed in first or second jobs.

Table 11: Resource Mobilization Matrix—Movement Against Toxic Mining

RESOURCES MOBILIZED IN SUPPORT OF KEY MOVEMENT TACTICS	STRATEGIC CAPABILITIES NEEDED	IMPACT ON MOVEMENT CHANCES OF SUCCESS
Tactic: Publicizing Dissent 1. **Specialist Labor** 50+ organizations & individuals writing & producing art or videos 2. **Cash & In-kind Contributions** Facebook page, computers, mural walls, video equipment 3. **Research & Information** Information on open-pit mining, water & the environment from FRECIUDAV, CEMDA, AIDA. 4. **Grants & Financing** Organizational budgets of NGOs, & grants from ICF, Packard, FASOL	**Unity** Strong degree of unity around threats from open-pit mining enabled translation by diverse organizations into entertaining & effective messages. **Strategy** A coordinating voice, FRECIUDAV, was important to define and support a series of tactics and protect the identities of movement participants. **Nonviolent Discipline** Maintenance of participant anonymity allowed wider participation with reduced threat of violent retaliation.	Mobilization of diverse capacities for messaging effectively grew movement participation across the state among the middle-class population. It has not effectively engaged poorer communities that seek the mining jobs.
Tactic: Use of Institutional Government Processes 1. **Volunteer Labor** Attendance at hearings & government consultation meetings around mining. 2. **Specialist Labor** Staff & organizational representatives from 50+ organizations preparing for & attending hearings & public meetings 3. **Research & Information** Information on open-pit mining, water & the environment from FRECIUDAV, CEMDA, AIDA.	**Unity** Participation of business and community leaders made social, economic & environmental arguments with clear agreement on movement demands to stop the *Los Cardones* project. **Strategy** Ability to formulate & disseminate strategy to discredit the permits and gain an official policy against toxic mining.	Exposed and promoted public accountability in municipal and state government officials and agencies, eventually forcing them to take a stand against the *Los Cardones* mine.
Tactic: Publicity, Declarations & Petitions 1. **Volunteer Labor** Individual volunteers for signing and collecting signatures 2. **Specialist Labor** FRECIUDAV, Todos Santos activists & AIDA writing & disseminating petitions 3. **Research & Information** Research & information on open-pit mining, water & the environment	**Unity** Shared experience in Todos Santos around demands to stop the dam. Coalition for the AIDA petition and ability to reach 50+ organizations with unified message. Weakness in reaching out to communities that rely on mining jobs. **Strategy** Pact of Todos Santos and AIDA petitions provided strategic outputs that were able to mobilize tens of thousands of volunteers to sign.	Carried movement messages into a local & national government, raising pressure on municipal, state and national government about citizen demands.
Tactic: Blockade of Roads & Occupation of Airports 1. **Volunteer Labor** Volunteer time for participation 2. **Cash & In-kind Contributions** Transport, food & communications	**Unity** The experience of past protests and demonstrations unified a core of activists to escalate demands and get sufficient participation in risky activities. **Strategy** Ability to respond rapidly allowed for the escalation and sustaining of the occupations until the governor of the state relented. **Nonviolence** Despite some reports of arguments with motorists and travelers, no violence reported.	Display of power energized core and raised the ability to influence government officials, including state governor and the new president of the country.

The movement made use of all five types of material resources identified in the monograph introduction (see Table 2): in-kind contributions; information and research; volunteer labor; specialized labor; and money. These resources were mobilized after the strategy and plans for resistance tactics became clear. In each instance, movement leaders focused on these tactics and not on the material resources that were required to execute them.

The movement's nonviolent tactics have included protests and demonstrations, publicizing dissent, resistance at government meetings, declarations and petitions, and a blockade of roads and occupation of airports. The section below follows Table 11 to elaborate in greater detail on the role of resources mobilized around the tactics chosen. We emphasize the tactics of publicizing dissent and the blockade and occupations because of the creativity of resources employed in the former and the uniqueness of the latter among the three movements we discuss in this monograph.

Publicizing Dissent

At the heart of the movement is the mobilization of active volunteer labor that brought a creative array of ways to publicize the movement's resistance to *Los Cardones* and, more broadly, to any toxic mining in the state. Highlights in the publicizing of dissent are the SOS demonstration (2011), the establishment of Facebook pages with at least 10,000 participants,[43] the production of pamphlets describing the effects of open-pit mining, the kayak demonstration in 2014, the painting of murals in La Paz, the Todos Santos Pact on September 12, 2014, and the over 211 articles produced in local and national media from 2011 to 2019 on opposition to *Los Cardones*.

As Figure 13 illustrates, the unified messages and the strategic participation of much of the population of Todos Santos enabled movement leaders to transform civic space, specialist labor, and volunteers into an enduring and quasi-official citizens proclamation to which references are still made today.

The **specialist labor** of movement organizations was critical for the production of pamphlets, such as "The Sierra La Laguna Mine: Ten things you should know," that give ready information debunking both misconceptions and arguments put forth by the mine investors. FRECIUDAV stressed that the most effective intervention has been providing people with this scientific and economic information about the project and the potential impacts of open-pit mining in a form they could use in public meetings. FRECIUDAV and other organizations such as SOS, Niparaja and *Agua Vale Más que el Oro* were important to the coordination

---

[43] As of December of 2019, FRECIUDAV's page has more than 14,000 likes, the closed group Movilización Civil Contra La Minería Baja California Sur (Civil Mobilization against Mining) has more than 5,000 members, and No a la Mineria Toxica en Baja California Sur (No to Toxic Mining) has over 4,000 members.

and logistics of publicity events such as the kayaking demonstration and the Todos Santos celebration.

Individuals providing **volunteer labor** also played a large role. Some painted murals that graphically depicted the dangers of mining, while others produced videos[44] and created performance art such as the creative messaging of the SOS demonstration in 2011, where thousands of state citizens contributed their physical bodies to form the letters of an SOS message. Organizations have often been able to mobilize more volunteers than they expected for their events. The SOS event is a good example, mobilizing many thousands more volunteers than expected by organizers to make the demonstration a success (Torres, 2011; Recuerda, 2011).

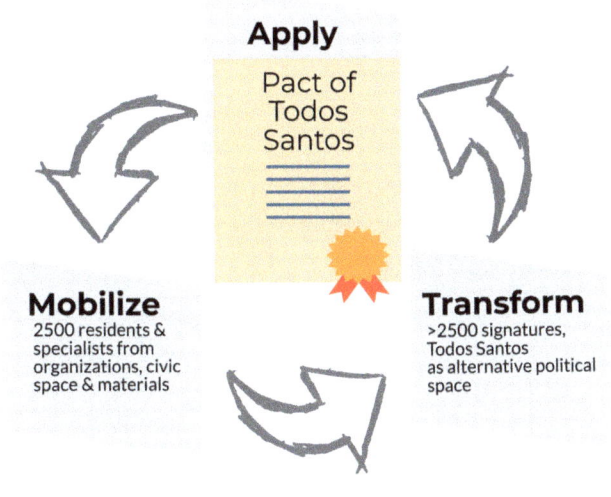

FIGURE 13: Circle of Resource Mobilization in BCS/Todos Santos

We do not have data on all of the roles played by local organizations for demonstrations, but almost all of the news articles point to the collaboration among multiple organizations for every event. We found the names of 25 local organizations mentioned in this context. FRECIUDAV stresses the distinctly home-grown organizational resources for the resistance to toxic mining in BCS and the wealth of research on which it can build: "We have the advantage of local centers of research and strong participation."[45]

One of the key capabilities that made it possible to mobilize and use these resources is a strong degree of **unity** among movement members around messaging. The unity around movement goals enabled mural artists, bloggers, and pamphlet writers—both among the 50+ collaborating organizations and as individual volunteers—to communicate the impacts of mining, which they did through entertaining and effective messaging. The establishment of FRECIUDAV helped create a **strategic** capacity to centralize some of the messaging through a movement spokesperson. Movement leaders stressed that it also helped to protect the time and identities of the various individuals and organizations, providing its loose coalition with a degree of anonymity and shielding them from reprisals. Given the extraordinary fear

---

44 YouTube has more than 100 videos uploaded by FRECIUDAV, MAS and other organizations between 2014 and 2018.

45 Movement Interview. La Paz, BCS, Mexico, by Skype, 10 Apr 2019.

of violence from opponents, security of members also helped to maintain and deepen **non-violent discipline** by keeping movement activities from responding to these reprisals.

The wide scope of collaborating organizations that includes community-based organizations, local and national environmental and rights NGOs, individuals, and even professional associations, has enabled the movement to craft a variety of messages aimed at a relatively wide audience. However, the interviews also pointed out one of the major capability-related weaknesses of the movement: its lack of unity with the mining communities in the mountains who support the reinstitution of mining. These communities tend to be economically depressed and benefit less from the state's booming tourism.

The mobilization of a significant swath of BCS's social and environmental specialist labor has largely had a positive impact on the movement. We heard there is stronger communication and shared cause among organizations. However, movement leaders stress the largely middle-class nature of this participation, without the poor communities, particularly in the old mining towns. In some cases, movement activists have transformed these strengthened linkages into new projects, creating an ongoing collaboration, as in the case of a new community center in La Paz in which mural artists from the movement are involved.[46] However, they are continuing to work in a context that can result in violent reprisal or mysterious disappearances, as the case of David Sosa who disappeared in 2011 illustrates.

Blockade of Roads and Occupation of Airports

By far, the most dramatic, risky and effective tactic of the BCS movement was the occupation of the transpeninsular road and the airports in San Jose del Cabo and La Paz that took place over three days in September of 2015. This was a significant action, since these are visible and important parts of the local tourist economy. In our interviews we could learn very little about the organization and execution of these events and most of our conclusions are drawn from news articles, our observations at the time, and information from people who were not centrally involved. Still some overall observations can be made.

The movement was able to mobilize hundreds of hours of **volunteer labor** from people who were capable of closing off the corridor for days and escalating this pressure by occupying the two regional airports (Figure 14). At the same time, it had sufficient **specialist labor** to make its public demands known as it waited on a response from the governor's office. Interviews showed that **in-kind contributions** came mainly from people self-financing their own transport, food and shelter needed for the events. There were no funds raised from **grants or financing,** but the ability of a few NGOs to provide labor and in-kind contributions was due to their own organizational financing.

---

[46] Movement Interview. La Paz, BCS, Mexico, by Skype, 10 Apr 2019.

In terms of capabilities, many of the activists blockading the roads and airports were veterans of past protests and demonstrations which gave them sufficient **unity** to escalate demands and gather enough people to make their activities a success. The ability to respond rapidly allowed for making **strategy** "on the fly," escalating and sustaining the occupations until the governor of the state relented. It is interesting to note that one activist in the blockade reported that "women were in the front taking a leading role in stopping traffic, while the men seemed to hang back on the outskirts."[47] This activist felt that having women in the front helped to reduce tempers and keep the peace. Despite some reports of arguments with motorists and travelers, the blockades and occupations maintained **nonviolent discipline**.

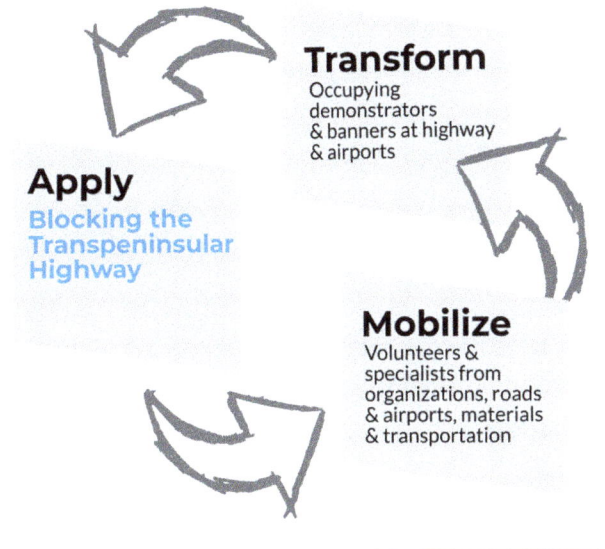

FIGURE 14: Circle of Resource Mobilization in BCS Highway

One of the major **impacts** of mobilizing members for a display of power in this way was the heightening of the movement's power to impact change. The governor of the state announced near the end of the occupations that the state would not accept the mining permits, reversing his earlier unwillingness to respond. The movement was able to voice its demands during the new president's first visit to the region. At the time the gold mining permits were still in question because the company had taken legal action in the courts to force the municipality of La Paz to abide by its original acceptance of the mining permits. While the president announced that he had to study the issue, months later on March 2 he announced that gold mining permits would not be allowed in the state.

Conclusions

The movement has mobilized significant material resources for its activities for over a decade from the specialist labor and communications resources of many organizations working in the state and nationally. One of the most effective things about this approach has been its ability to respond rapidly to the company's moves in diverse ways—from demonstrations and occupations to policy arguments.

---

47   Movement Interview. Pescadero, BCS, Mexico, 25 May 2019.

The mobilization of "middle class" resources that came from established organizations and as part of educated labor, however, has also come with some drawbacks. The movement has not effectively brought in the poorer communities in the old mining towns of the Sierra, many of whom acutely feel the loss of mining jobs. As the state grapples with the wins of the movement, it is hard to say where these fractures will lead. Movement leaders believe that the struggle against toxic mining is still up against major economic powers in the country that will not relent.

While there was little direct support for movement activities from national and international grantmaking organizations such as the Packard Foundation and the International Community Foundation, grantmakers have supported many of the collaborating organizations. This funding has contributed to the strength of NGO budgets ranging from large organizations (Niparajá) to the many smaller organizations that comprise the movement. FASOL has also been operating in the region for over a decade providing small grants more directly to movement activities. This specialist labor supported by NGO budgets that characterized the resources mobilized in BCS shaped the way it was able to be nimble and rapidly spread around the state.

4. Aquí ¡No!: Stopping an Ammonia Plant, Sinaloa

Overview of the Movement

In 2013 the residents of the state of Sinaloa heard that a plant to produce ammonia for agricultural fertilizer was to be constructed on the shores of the Bay of Ohuira, in Topolobampo. *Gas y Petroquímica de Occidente SA de CV* (known locally as GPO, a Mexican subsidiary of the Swiss-German engineering, procurement and construction group Proman AG) announced plans to construct a plant capable of producing 2,200 metric tons of fertilizer per year.

To local residents, this announcement came as a surprise, since the entire lagoon system of Topolobampo–Ohuira–Santa María had been declared a protected Ramsar site[48] in 2009, which did not seem to factor into plans for the project. The plant and accompanying transport infrastructure would cover 200 hectares of productive wetland. Local residents and scientists noted that this area serves as a refuge and breeding center for shrimp, sea lions, bottlenose dolphins, fish, crabs, and sea turtles, which use the area as a feeding ground and are

FIGURE 15: Map of Topolobampo, Sinaloa

---

48   A Ramsar site is a wetland site designated to be of international importance under The Convention on Wetlands, known as the Ramsar Convention, which is an intergovernmental environmental treaty established in 1971 by UNESCO. It provides for national action and international cooperation regarding the conservation of wetlands and wise sustainable use of their resources.

permanent residents of the Ramsar site. There is an active fishing industry, and at one time it was the primary source of shrimp exported to the United States. Tourism is also quite active, and many residents of the nearby towns make a living from tourists who come for dolphin watching, bird watching, and water sports (see Figure 15).

Yet on April 21, 2014, the General Directorate of Environmental Impact and Risk, a department of Mexico's Ministry of the Environment and Natural Resources (SEMARNAT), approved the company's Environmental Impact Statement and authorized construction of the plant.[49] Construction began in 2015 with a platform of 20 hectares constructed on the wetland. Since then, the project has proceeded to start and stop several times as citizens fight it in court, in the media, and in the streets and waterways.

Despite local concern, there was no visible opposition to the project until June of 2015, when three events came together to raise the public profile of the project. First, as company construction workers began pulling out mangrove trees and filling in the wetland, local fishermen landed on the shore and confronted the construction superintendent. In the same month, the Federal Congressman[50] Gerardo Peña Avilés publicly challenged the legality of the project. He held two meetings with company officials to discuss the project. Failing to dissuade the company from carrying on with the project, he joined up with a local residents' group, the Residents Committee of Topolobampo,[51] to call on the local fishermen to mount a large mobilization against the project. The mobilization was blocked when the fishermen were threatened, and the company said it would sue the congressman.

These actions raised awareness about the project. Local fishermen, tourist operators, restaurant owners, and scientists were all alarmed by the project, and began to inform themselves about the plans. One fishing cooperative member observed: "How can I permit someone to come from outside and harm my work when I am my own boss? People have been fishing here for 120 years in this community."[52]

Over the next two years concerned organizations and individuals created a strategic campaign to challenge the ammonia plant (see Table 12 for types of organizations involved in the movement). As part of that campaign, opponents saw that a key piece would be to challenge the plant in court, since by law there were many regulatory hurdles the company needed to overcome. Members of the campaign filed three separate lawsuits. One was based

---

49   Autorización en materia de impacto ambiental con Resolutivo de Impacto Ambiental No. GPA/DGIRA/DG/03576, de fecha 21 de abril del 2014, expedido por la Dirección General de Impacto y Riesgo Ambiental de la Semarnat.

50   Diputado Federal.

51   El Comité Único de la Vivienda de Topolobampo.

52   Movement Interview. Lázaro Cárdenas, Sinaloa, Mexico, 9 May 2019.

on violations of Mexican environmental law, and two were based on lack of consultation with Indigenous communities to get their free prior and informed consent, required under Mexican and international law for projects wherever Indigenous communities live. All three suits were initially upheld by the courts, stopping the project.

Table 12: Principal Organizations in the Aquí ¡No! Movement

PRINCIPAL ORGANIZATIONS IN THE MOVEMENT	
TYPE	**ORGANIZATION**
COMMUNITY ORGANIZING	
Community Based Organization	Residents of Lazaro Cardenas
Community Based Organization	Residents Committee of Topolobampo
Cooperative	Cooperative of Tourist Operators of Topolobampo
Cooperative	Pavedones Fishing cooperative
Cooperative	Lagoon of Ohuira Fishing cooperative
Ejido (local government)	Ejido of Lazaro Cardenas
Federation of Cooperatives	21st Federation of Fishermen
Private Sector Federation	Federation de Restaurants in Topolobampo
INDIGENOUS PEOPLES RIGHTS	
Indigenous governance	Supreme Council of Kobanaros and Yoremes Mayos Indigenous Peoples of Sinaloa
ENVIRONMENTAL RESEARCH AND ACTION	
Academic	National Polytechnic Institute
Government research organization	Center for Interdisciplinary Research on Integrated Regional Development (IPN CIIDIR)
Network (Campaign Coordination)	*Aquí ¡No!* Not Here!
NGO	Citizens Parliament of Culiacán
NGO	Save the Forest Council (Culiacán) (*Bosque a Salvo*)
NGO	Citizens Ecology Council of Sinaloa (Culiacán)
NGO	National Citizens Congress Los Mochis
FUNDING	
International Foundation	The Ford Foundation
Domestic Foundation	Action in Solidarity Fund (*Fondo Acción Solidaria*)

Yet the limitations of this institutional tactic became evident just after the courts ruled against the plant on October 15, 2018. The lawsuit had been brought by Librado Bacasegua Elenes, President of the Supreme Council of Kobanaros and Yoremes Mayos Indigenous Peoples of Sinaloa. In a seemingly strange turn of events, he then withdrew his name from the lawsuit the day after he had won. Because the suit was brought on the basis of the

Supreme Council of Kobanaros and Yoremes Mayos Indigenous Peoples of Sinaloa, and not him individually, the injunction remained in force, but the Council was divided. Local press reports at the time noted that:

> To do so, he resorted to the law firm *Lozada y Asociados*, and concealed the fact from his lawyer representative in the injunction, Máximo Montes, and the collective *Aquí ¡No!*, which supported him. Kobanaro clan advisors stated that Librado was being pressured by politicians, related lawyers and business mediators to such an extent that he accepted the construction of a branch road to his community, a health clinic, a new truck and 1.5 million pesos to give up [the lawsuit] (Najera, Rio Doce, November 27, 2018).

The situation was then made more complex when a third lawsuit was brought by another Indigenous leader in November 2018, based on similar arguments that Indigenous people were not consulted in the development of the project. On November 21, the Sixth District court granted the temporary injunction.

Campaign activists intertwined their legal challenges with civil resistance tactics to show the level of local concern, and to bring pressure on the courts to rule in the public interest, and not just the interests of the company.

The legal process has been complicated and contested, but to date it has blocked the project from proceeding. Campaign activists intertwined their legal challenges with civil resistance tactics to show the level of local concern, and to bring pressure on the courts to rule in the public interest, and not just the interests of the company. At the same time, the Citizens Ecology Council of Sinaloa, an NGO based in the state capital Culiacan, held several more meetings with the company, again with no results.

Aquí ¡No!: The Coalition Organizes

By the end of 2017 these independent actions—meetings with company staff, public protests and lawsuits—came together, united in common cause. A combination of environmental groups, fishermen's cooperatives, and local tourist businesses joined forces to fight the project. Leadership came from the congressman, the local fishermen's cooperatives, Indigenous councils, and a small environmental NGO in the state capital, Bosque a Salvo. Bosque a Salvo is a small volunteer-run NGO that took the lead in bringing these constituencies together. It introduced more unified planning and strategy to the movement. Together they created a leadership council that meets from time to time to review progress and plan future actions. The coalition united around a theme of *"Aquí ¡No!"*, that is, "Not Here!" This branding unified the campaign, pulling together a diversity of interests and goals into an easy-to-remember theme (see flyer in Figure 16). This diverse group came together around common goals, despite the differences in interests and styles of the members.

Activities picked up as a result, both in appealing to state institutions—courts, legislature, and the president—and outside these institutions, in the form of protests and a communications campaign to reframe the issue from jobs and progress to destruction of the fishing industry and health threats to residents. At the same time, technical studies by the Center for Interdisciplinary Research on Integrated Regional Development (IPN CIIDIR), a government research institute, supported the concerns of the movement, adding legitimacy to the campaign.

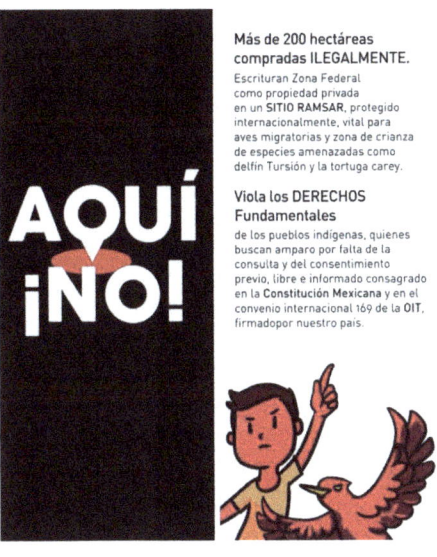

FIGURE 16: "Aquí ¡No!" Campaign Information Flyer

Protests took different forms. Sports figures lent their names to the movement, one by swimming across the bay, another by windsurfing in it, all with videos, publicity, and *Aquí ¡No!* banners in full view. Fishermen staged protests in their boats in front of the plant site, again with large banners and television and press coverage, and later the collective organized other protests on land (see Topolabampo demonstration in Figure 17). The movement intentionally chose key times for these protests: the opening of the highway into town when the state governor was present for the ceremony, on National Marine Day when government officials again were present, and on the road from the airport when the Mexican president came to visit the region. In the case of the president, campaigners organized to stop his car and hand him documents pleading their case, with 800 mobilized citizens behind them.

In all cases, media presence was high, and the campaign documented everything on Facebook[53] and through news reports on YouTube.[54] They organized themselves to have a designated spokesman, and prepared printed materials, banners, t-shirts, and stickers for use at every event. The *Aquí ¡No!* campaign also organized several press conferences. Campaigners found that if press conferences were called by their state legislative representatives, press attendance was much improved, and the campaign gained legitimacy.

Many of the members of *Aquí ¡No!* organized their own communities behind these protests and publicity events. Table 13 provides a timeline of activities.

---

53 Facebook page: **https://www.facebook.com/AQU%C3%8D-NO-colectivo-ecologico-2171978103072980/**

54 For an example from YouTube: **https://www.youtube.com/watch?v=CLILBcATmfQ**.

FIGURE 17: Demonstration in Topolobampo. The t-shirts and banner were paid for by a movement member.

Used with permission.

Indigenous groups held meetings explaining the project to community members and encouraging them to support the movement. One woman organized community theater in her Indigenous language of Yoreme about the issue and performed around the area to raise awareness. The fishing cooperatives, which are very strong in the area, educated their members, and continued to use funds from membership dues to support legal expenses to pursue the lawsuits. This community organizing became even more important when the company began circulating through the area dispensing funds and goods to build good will and convert opponents to supporters. "GPO is seeding discord in the community," lamented one community leader. "They want to change our natural resources and way of life."[55] Another observed:

> GPO has given support to the schools. It has supported the treatment of illness, the payment of pensions. They brought sweets on the 'Day of the Child.' In general, they are doing social work... it is not bad to help the community, but when they get involved in corrupting people it is dangerous.[56]

Local marine science academics from IPN CIIDIR, a government research institute, who were initially involved in doing the Environmental Impact Statement lent their expertise to the movement, providing critiques of company documents, supplying arguments to the movement spokesperson, and supporting the lawsuits.

One of the most effective institutional tactics has been taking the company to court. The principle source of material support for this work has been the 21st Century Federation of Fishermen. The Federation as a matter of course has a lawyer hired on retainer, and it has used his time to bring its cases to court. The Federation has used two different lawyers, since the first one changed sides under pressure and incentives from the company. In addition to lawyers' fees, the Federation has also covered expenses needed for the lawyers' travel to the state and federal capitals to attend hearings. As of March 2020, legal action continued to prevent the company from carrying out the project.

---

55   Movement Interview. Lázaro Cárdenas, Sinaloa, Mexico, 9 May 2019.

56   Movement Interview. Topolobampo, Sinaloa, Mexico, 10 Jun 2019.

Over time, the coalition saw that legal action alone may be insufficient, since there were no guarantees that courts would continue to rule in their favor, or that plaintiffs would not be bought off by the company. The coalition made sure that its strategy included continuing to organize communities and to mount demonstrations, press conferences, and publicity campaigns with the aim to expand public support for the communities and reduce the chances that state institutions like the courts and the Environment Ministry would rule against them. While legal action is more of an institutional tactic than a civil resistance tactic, movement leaders have seen the need to pursue both approaches simultaneously.

Further support and funding for campaign activities came from the NGOs based in Culiacán, the state capital. Support for communications and legal strategies also came from FASOL, through funding from the Ford Foundation in Mexico City and New York, in the form of a workshop and technical assistance for socioenvironmental groups across the country on how to use the courts to support community struggles.

Table 13: Timeline of the Aquí ¡No! Movement

		TIMELINE OF THE AQUÍ ¡NO! MOVEMENT
2013		Project proposed by Gas y Petroquímica de Occidente SA de CV (GPO)
2014	21 April	Environmental Impact Assessment approved
2015	June	Construction began
	June	Fishermen blockaded the shore and confront construction supervisor
		Federal Congressman Gerardo Peña Avilés and a group of fishermen met privately with company officials
		The United Committee of Topolobampo Residents and Congressman Peña called for a massive mobilization against the plant
		News reporter Gabriela Soto and her team published an exposé of government corruption in the state. She was fired soon after.
2016	April	Court order to the environmental protection agency Profepa (Federal Agency for Environmental Protection, *Procuraduría Federación de Protección al Ambiente*) to halt construction, arguing that the project would cause environmental damage
	June	The Mexican Senate asked the head of the SEMARNAT to suspend the project
	September	Profepa completed its court-ordered inspection of the project and approved it
2017	December	Ecological collective *Aquí ¡No!* created
2018	June	First press conference by the *Aquí ¡No!* Collective, held in the State Congress Small demonstrations in the public square in Topolobampo
	September	María Esther Hinojosa swam across the Bay of Ohuira to raise awareness
	15 October	District Court ruled in favor of Indigenous group, issued an injunction. Indigenous leader withdrew his name from petition 18 hours later
	November	Martín García Cruz filed in court for a separate injunction against the project Fishermen staged protest in front of plant
2019	March	District court granted injunction against the plant to *Ejido El Muellecito* on environmental grounds Two demonstrations in Quijote Plaza in Topolobampo
	June	Demonstration on Marine Day
	June	Large demonstration for arrival of Mexican President Andrés Manuel López Obrador
	July	Press conference by the *Aquí ¡No!* Collective

How Material Resources Were Mobilized and Used by the Movement

Table 14 summarizes the role of material resources in the movement. The main civil resistance tactics developed by movement leaders and the material resources used in support of them are in the left column. The capabilities that the movement needed to generate and use those resources and the resulting effects on movement capacity appear in the second and third columns.

Table 14: Resource Mobilization Matrix—Aquí ¡No!

RESOURCES MOBILIZED IN SUPPORT OF KEY MOVEMENT TACTICS	STRATEGIC CAPABILITIES NEEDED	IMPACT ON MOVEMENT CHANCES OF SUCCESS
Tactic: Community Organizing 1. <u>In-kind contributions:</u> Transport: fishermen made their boats available for free to transport Aquí ¡No! representatives to meet with local communities to educate them and solidify support 2. <u>Volunteers:</u> Aquí ¡No! volunteers gave their time for these meetings 3. <u>Research & information:</u> local scientists presented technical information	**Unity** Organizational structure to hold well-attended meetings Reframing of issue to protection of fisheries, tourism, and human health **Strategy** Choice of key communities to organize Use of local leaders for each community	Solidified initial community support. Reliance on volunteer labor limited the ability to counter the campaigning at the community level by company staff
Tactic: Demonstrations 1. <u>In-kind contributions:</u> 2. Transport: fishermen made their boats available for free and people volunteered their cars to transport people to demonstrations 3. <u>Volunteers:</u> Aquí ¡No! volunteers gave their time for these demonstrations 4. <u>Cash:</u> used for printing leaflets, banners, stickers 5. <u>Research & information:</u> local scientists presented technical information	**Strategy** Leaders chose moments of highest visibility and discomfort to political leaders **Discipline** No incidents of violence took place, even during blockades, or in the face of corruption or illegal activity by company staff	Use of in-kind contributions, cash and volunteers enabled the movement to demonstrate wide public support and influence government decision-making.
Tactic: Use of Institutional Government Processes 1. <u>Cash:</u> The fishermen's coops used their lawyer and cash contributions from members to support legal fees and transportation 2. <u>Research & information:</u> local scientists presented technical information used in court documents 3. <u>Grants:</u> Training by FASOL built movement capacity to use courts	**Strategy** Movement leaders cooperated in different groups using different legal strategies to complicate company attempts to counter them Movement leaders used public demonstrations to show courts the degree of support for the cases **Discipline** Maintaining nonviolent tactics lent legitimacy to legal challenges	The ready access to the Fishermen's Federation lawyer and the cash to support him made lawsuits a natural tactic. Early success with this tactic may have delayed grassroots organizing when the legal cases faced difficulties
Tactic: Publicity and Information 1. <u>Grants:</u> US$3000 from FASOL supported production of videos to generate community and public support 2. <u>Cash:</u> contributions supported printing of materials and banners, and a billboard for one month 3. <u>Specialist Labor:</u> donated logo and materials design, scientists interpreted technical documents 4. <u>Volunteer labor:</u> all materials produced by volunteer labor, press conferences done by movement members and their legislative representatives	**Unity** Common agreement on messages **Strategy** Public messaging campaigns consistent across media: Facebook, YouTube, printed materials, billboard, press conferences	Access to many free or cheap outlets for messaging: Use of social media, access to legislators, sympathetic press, cynicism about politicians and local education events all gave the movement an edge over the company which had far more money

The movement made use of all five types of material resources identified in the monograph introduction (see Table 2 on page 28): Volunteer Labor, Specialist Labor (including skills and knowledge of people), Cash and In-Kind Contributions, Research and Information, and Grants and Financing. These resources were mobilized after the strategy and plans for resistance tactics became clear. In each instance, movement leaders focused on these tactics and not on the material resources that were required for them. The following sections expand on these uses for two of the most important tactics—publicity and information sharing and demonstrations—to illustrate their role in the movement.

Publicity and Information Sharing

The movement has been able to use free and low-cost materials and outlets to disseminate its messages. The resources to craft these messages and get them out broadly were:

Grants: Grants for movement groups are rare, yet contacts with FASOL produced two grants in 2018, one for US$3000 for the production of videos to generate community and public support, and a second for US$3000 to support community theater to mobilize people against the plant in Indigenous communities. Both grants were made to an NGO from the capital, Bosque a Salvo.

Cash: Contributions from members and a small number of outside supporters paid for the printing of materials, t-shirts and banners, and a billboard displayed for one month on the main road into town. These materials gave a visible presence to the movement obvious to all in the area, and those who saw reports in the press and on television news.

Specialist Labor: Some professionals donated their time to creating a logo and designing the printed materials and banners. Government funding for IPN CIIDIR, a government research institute, supported scientists who challenged company documents and studies.

Volunteer labor: All materials were produced by volunteer labor, and the numerous press conferences were done by movement members and their legislative representatives. Movement leaders found that the press was more attracted to press conferences called by legislators, so they teamed up with their representatives to present press conferences together and get out the movement messages to a wider audience.

As a result of these resources and their strategic use, the movement has had considerable success in generating coverage in television and print media, with articles appearing in numerous outlets. *Meganoticias*, a Mexican news TV channel, has been especially interested in the case. Some of this coverage has been unsolicited, but the movement has also done well in seeking out opportunities for media coverage.

Social media has been a primary outlet for movement communication, especially Facebook. The *Aquí ¡No! – colectivo ecologico* Facebook page has 2,391 followers (as of March 20, 2021), and posts videos, positions, announcements, and updates every day. Interestingly, the rival Facebook page set up by the company has few followers, and most posts there are from *Aquí ¡No!* followers.

The coalition has also developed flyers, posters, bumper stickers, and t-shirts for the cause, all using the *Aquí ¡No!* logo developed by a local graphic designer who donated her time to do it (see Figure 16). The 21st Century Federation of Fishermen also used its own funds to pay for a billboard for one month on the only road into town publicizing the dangers of an ammonia accident to the region (see Figure 18).

FIGURE 18: Billboard Showing Consequences of an Ammonia Spill in the Area

One movement leader noted that "The most important resource is getting our message out. It is the strength of the whole movement because if people are not informed nothing will happen."

What capabilities were needed or lacking to mobilize these resources? Creating **unity** across the movement and expanding the number of followers required the development of a shared and inclusive framing of the issues. The movement could have focused solely on the environmental issues, but instead it broadened its message to appeal to fishermen, Indigenous people, and local tourism operators, which helped it to acquire cash, volunteers and specialist labor that were utilized in the dissemination of its messages. In contrast to the company and government's message of new jobs and support to local farmers, the movement recast the issue as a threat to thousands of fishing and tourism jobs and a health threat to everyone in the area.

In addition, the movement held periodic press conferences in June of 2018 and July of 2019. Strategically the movement held these press conferences in the state capital Culiacan, rather than in the smaller towns affected by the plant. Contacts with sympathetic state legislatures were key to drawing press attendance.

Good **strategic planning** by the movement council ensured consistency of messages across media: Facebook, YouTube, printed materials, billboard, press conferences.

What is the **impact** of the way material resources are allocated and used on a movement's chances of success or failure? In this case access to "free" resources—Facebook, YouTube, press conferences—has allowed the movement to effectively counter company messages, despite the company's vastly larger budget for publicity. For materials that had to be purchased—printed materials, t-shirts, a billboard—the council was able to get members to donate the cash needed to purchase them at strategic times.

Demonstrations

A key tactic for the movement has been to organize public demonstrations. The first public manifestation of dissent was mounted spontaneously by fishermen in anger over the beginning of the plant's construction in June of 2015. Yet as the movement increased its organizational capacity, these demonstrations became more planned and strategic. In November of 2018 fishermen and tourist operators from the towns of Topolobampo and Lázaro Cárdenas staged a protest in their boats in the harbor, while others demonstrated in the town's main Plaza Quijote, all with *Aquí ¡No!* t-shirts and banners visible. The council mounted two more demonstrations in 2019, one on National Marine Day, and the second on the day the president came to visit the area.

The resources that were mobilized to support the demonstrations were:

1. In-kind contributions: One of the main needs of the movement was transport to get people to demonstrations at the right time and in sufficient numbers. Fishermen made their boats available for free, and people volunteered their cars to transport people to demonstrations. Leaders organized transport by word of mouth and through Facebook, giving times and locations.

2. Volunteers: Numbers of participants at demonstrations varied from a few dozen to 800 people, all volunteers. Organizing the events, distributing t-shirts, fliers, and banners, and communicating messages was all done by *Aquí ¡No!* volunteers giving their time.

3. Cash: This was important to buy needed materials used for printing leaflets, banners, and stickers. The majority of cash came from the tourist operators and a few outside supporters. Amounts were modest and generated in response to need—there was no explicit fundraising in which movement leaders asked for cash to support movement activities.

4. Research & information: Since the project was of a very technical nature, it was crucial for the movement to understand and counter technical arguments about how safe the project was for the local environment and people. Local scientists provided technical information and analysis both to movement leaders, who then used them in their speeches at demonstrations, and in the media interviews that occurred at each event.

FIGURE 19: Circle of Resource Mobilization in Sinaloa

What movement capabilities were critical to mobilize and make use of resources? Good strategic planning was key. Leaders chose moments of highest visibility and discomfort to political leaders. After the first spontaneous demonstration in 2015, the council planned all demonstrations for key moments when political decision makers were present. In two of the cases, the state governor was in attendance for "feel good" photo opportunities that the demonstrations undermined, creating a difficult situation for the governor to manage. The council also ensured that considerable press was present for all events, provided videos and photos through social media, and made both its spokesperson and former congressman available for press interviews.

A second movement capability that was key was the maintenance of **nonviolent discipline**. No incidents of violence took place, even during blockades or in the face of corruption or illegal activity by company staff. As Figure 19 illustrates, a nonviolent, high visibility strategy enabled movement leaders to transform the harbor, boats and leaflets into a demonstration that got the attention of government leaders.

What Is the Impact of the Way Material Resources Are Allocated and Used on a Movement's Chances of Success or Failure?

Use of in-kind contributions, cash and volunteers enabled the movement to demonstrate wide public support and influence government decision-making. On the other hand, the movement has experienced greater difficulty in preventing defections of key local leaders involved in the legal process. The company's response to legal setbacks was to make large amounts of money available both to individuals and communities, which has been difficult for the movement to counter. The movement's inability to match the 10.8 million pesos (US$540,000) available in 2018 alone resulted in division as some members defected to take the company's offers of cash, vehicles, trips, and community services. The movement's decision not to pursue cash fundraising has left it vulnerable to this tactic.

Conclusions

In Sinaloa, the movement did not generate resources ahead of time and stock them for future use. As the council of *Aquí ¡No!* decided on the next tactic, it then generated resources among its own members to pull it off. The collective did not raise or gather these resources centrally—once a tactic was agreed on, each part of the collective brought what resources it could and deployed them directly. Early success with legal challenges emphasized the value for the movement of specialist labor and cash to support it. Over time, the council saw that this institutional tactic had its limits, and the greater resources of the company and politicians made it unlikely that this tactic alone would win the day. Beginning in 2018 the council increased its emphasis on organizing communities, educating them about the project, warning them about attempts by the company to buy off members, and encouraging local leadership, especially among the fishermen and Indigenous communities. Its shrewd use of publicity at low cost and wide distribution—through both social media and independent press and television outlets—built support for the cause and reduced the likelihood of backroom deals between the company, the courts, and the Environment Ministry.

This non-hierarchical unity gave the sense that the movement was speaking for the public good as opposed to isolated self-interest

To do this, the movement needed the capacity to generate appealing messages and disseminate them consistently through the different constituencies that made them up. Discipline in avoiding violent tactics was consistent, though it was rarely an issue in the campaign. And finally, the non-hierarchical nature of the movement made it hard for opponents to accuse the movement of simply pursuing self-interest: fishermen, environmentalists, scientists, tourist operators, and resident associations all spoke from their differing perspectives, yet with mutually supporting themes. This non-hierarchical unity gave the sense that the movement was speaking for the public good as opposed to isolated self-interest.

5. Implications for Movements

Our research shows that movement leaders are astute in matching their resource mobilization to their tactical needs in the changing contexts they face. In this way, we believe the lessons around resource mobilization from the three movements discussed in this paper will be familiar to movement leaders in many countries.

The lessons here can help movement leaders and supporters—researchers, funders, support organizations—to plan and strategize about the material resources they need. And we hope that these lessons will demonstrate that it is inaccurate to characterize movements as resource poor. In Mexico, while they did not have access to a ready reserve of money, these movements proved quite capable of attracting what they needed and transforming it to effectively create and amplify their messages. Furthermore, these messages proved to be a formidable power against significantly better resourced opponents.

The implications, which we discuss below, are thus intended to help understand, plan, and carry out strategies in ways which, in our experience, many movement leaders already are thinking about. We hope they can also be useful for others sympathetic to movement goals, whether support organizations, policy makers, or funders.

1. **Volunteer labor is a key resource for movements.** Volunteers contribute their bodies and voices to public demonstrations, their time to movement activities, and their cash and in-kind resources to nearly all activities. But more than this, they become a force within the movement for aligning strategies and for keeping the movement responsive to diverse needs. Since most of their activities are self-financed, movement activities can often happen without a lot of pre-planning to take advantage of a political opportunity or a public event.

2. **Strategy and tactics drive resource mobilization.** These three movements did not generate resources independent of their tactics. Leaders developed strategies and tactics and then gathered resources to support them. At the same time, strategies and tactics were constrained by the resources available—in no case did leaders develop strategies that required things they could not get. This lack of a resource mobilization infrastructure does not appear to be a cultural or context-specific attribute particular to the three movements we researched, but integral to the way in which movements generally are able to respond to strategic or political opportunities as they emerge. Having said that, larger, more formal civil society organizations that

support these movements *do* need to raise outside resources to pay staff or conduct activities.

3. **Maintenance of nonviolent discipline and the use of nonviolent actions draw support and brought in more people and a more diverse range of resources.** In a very violent context where resources are contested by criminal forces as well as companies and government mega-projects, the maintenance of nonviolence in the face of reprisals and threats is remarkable. As one movement leader in Nayarit said, it is not the *principle* of nonviolence that movements relied on, but its *strategic importance*. "Of course, if our homes or family are threatened, we will defend ourselves, however we can."[57] From the security considerations in Baja to the solidarity organizing with Indigenous peoples in Nayarit and Sinaloa, it was clear that nonviolence was practiced everywhere as an unspoken understanding.

4. **Funders support movements best through clear and specific strategies at the right level.** While frontline movements received little money from outside funders, foundations and government agencies nevertheless provided crucial support to the wider movement. Funding for larger, more formal institutions like NGOs and government departments provided expertise to the movement in communications, law, technical studies, and advocacy that made a big difference in movement success.

   Foundations can provide funds to frontline organizations, as FASOL and ICF did, yet they do not have to do so to make valuable contributions. Whether funding goes to frontline organizations or to other more formal support organizations, funders support the movement best when they see themselves as part of it. Regular consultations with movement leaders can inform funders of what the movement needs, and allow them to tailor their support to movement strategy, even when the funding goes to larger support organizations. Funders do best when they understand the ecosystem of movement organizations and the strategies they are pursuing. Funders like FASOL that are set up to provide funding to frontline organizations can support them directly, but larger foundations and government departments must work with more bureaucratic restrictions, which makes them less helpful at that level. At the same time, their ability to support the more formal organizations far outstrips that of grassroots funders. This combination of funding support at all levels is what most movements need to succeed.

5. **Movement members and tactics endow resources with meaning.** That is, what movement leaders consider a useful resource depends on who it is coming from and

---

[57] Movement Interview. Ruiz, Nayarit, Mexico, 26 Apr 2019.

what it can mean for carrying out a civil resistance tactic. A vehicle has no meaning until it is driven to a meeting or demonstration or it is given to movement leaders to buy them off. In these three cases, volunteer time represented sacrifice by movement members on behalf of the larger cause, which were framed as "David vs. Goliath" battles over basic rights to life and livelihood. Scientific analyses became relevant when movements framed their struggles as environmental. In the cases where Indigenous communities were threatened in Sinaloa and Nayarit, cultural arguments and legal requirements for consultation became relevant.

At the same time, a grant from a funder like FASOL, which is seen as part of the movement, is more acceptable to movement leaders than the same amount of money from companies or government agencies. Movement leaders see some sympathetic funders as part of their movements, thanks to a chain of trust built over the years.

6. **Each successful application of a resource can open up new resources.** Movement activities add value not only to their specific campaigns and tactics, but also in motivating people to bring in new labor, goods, and money that can be mobilized for their next series of tactics, or for like causes. As public dialogues along the San Pedro River progressed, the communities were motivated to devote their labor, goods, and money to fight for rights and environmental causes. Victory against the *Los Cardones* mine led BCS citizens to be more supportive of their robust sector of social and environmental organizations.

7. **Resources can be raised and used in a decentralized way**. While messages may be created in a unified way across a movement, raising resources occurs in a decentralized way, with each part drawing on its constituencies and expertise to generate and use volunteer time, professional services, cash and in-kind contributions, and information in ways that make the most sense for them. Movements make use of a large organizational infrastructure, but resources come from the individuals and organizations who are part of it.

8. **Formal organizations are important as channels for the resources that movements need, particularly cash, information and specialized skills**. They pay the salaries for the specialist labor that the movement needs to coordinate, make, or deliver the products—from pamphlets to dialogues—that are so important to success. These movements each had central coordinating groups that could set the strategy, but they relied on many individuals and organizations to raise, receive, and spend money independently in line with that strategy.

These movements mobilized significant resources, despite informal organization and significant opposition. We did not find significant resources coming from foundations or other philanthropic sources for frontline groups, but grants to national and international NGOs served an important function in supporting specialist labor in research and advocacy. Organizations that want to support movements could become more effective in their work if they move beyond transactional support for discrete projects and focus more on facilitating the development of social processes. Supporting movement capabilities, organizational links, and ability to access resources can generate lasting social change. Foundations, large NGOs, and other movement support organizations improve their ability to promote promising movements by understanding that successful movements rapidly transform the material resources at hand into tactical resistance in support of long-term strategies.

Bibliography

Ackerman, Peter and Hardy Merriman. "The Checklist for Ending Tyranny." In *Is Authoritarianism Staging a Comeback?*, edited by Mathew Burrows and Maria J. Stephan. Washington, DC: The Atlantic Council, 2015.

Aguayo, S. "AMLO y las OSC." *Reforma,* March 13, 2019. Accessed November 15, 2019. https://www.cemefi.org/servicios/noticias/filantropicas/5391-amlo-y-las-osc-articulo-de-sergio-aguayo-publicado-en-reforma.html

Aguilar, Alberto. "CFE por 3 Hidroeléctricas Simultáneas, pronto Las Cruces en Nayarit, Chicoasén II el Viernes y Avanzan 5 Termoeléctricas." *Milenio,* June 1, 2019.

Alinsky, Saul David. *Rules for Radicals: A Practical Primer for Realistic Radicals.* New York: Vintage Books, 1971.

Allan, Chris and A. Scott DuPree. "Resilient Funders: How Funders are Adapting to the Closing Space for Civil Society." *The Foundation Review,* 10, no. 2 (June 2018).

Almeida, P. and A. Cordero, eds. *Movimientos Sociales en América Latina: Perspectivas, Tendencias y Casos.* Buenos Aires: CLACSO, 2017.

Almeyra, Guillermo. "Los Vaivenes de los Movimientos Sociales en México." *OSAL* IX, no. 24, (October 2008) 87-101.

Alonso, Jorge and Juan Manuel Ramírez, eds. *La Democracia de los Abajo en Jalisco.* Guadalajara: Universidad of Guadalajara, 1996.

Alonso, Jorge, ed. *Los Movimientos Sociales en el Valle de México.* Vol. 2, Mexico City: CIESAS. Mexico, 1988.

Alonso, Jorge, ed. *Identidades, Acción Colectiva y Movimientos Sociales.* Zapopan: El Colegio de Jalisco, 2001.

Alonso, Jorge. *En Busca de la Convergencia: El Partido Obrero Campesino Mexicano.* Mexico City: CIESAS, 1990.

Alonso, Jorge. "Una Revisión Somera de los Movimientos Sociales Mexicanos." Accessed November 18, 2019. https://www.nodo50.org/ceprid/spip.php?article1343

Ávila Carillo, Enrique. *Movimientos y Conflictos Sociales en México 1943-2011.* Mexico: ¡Uníos!, 2011.

Aziz, Alberto, and Jorge Alonso. *México, una Semocracia Vulnerada.* Mexico City: CIESAS, 2009.

Baja Post. "AMLO Cancels Los Cardones Mine Project in BCS." *The Baja Post,* March 4, 2019.

Barry, Jenny. "La Organización entre Movimientos en México Conduce a Nuevos Recursos." Accessed December 1, 2019. https://www.openglobalrights.org/cross-movement-organizing-in-mexico-leads-to-new-resources/

Bartra, Armando, J.E. Beltrán, J. Cárdenas, L. Concheiro, A. Córdova, A. Díaz Lastra, H. Díaz Polanco, L Esquivel, V. Flores Olea, L.J. Garrido, *et al. Nuevo Proyecto de Nación. Por el Renacimiento de México*, Mexico: Grijalbo Mondadori, 2011.

BCS Noticias. "Ciudadanos Buscan Impedir la Construcción de una Desaladora Relacionada con Los Cardones." *BCS Noticias,* September 4, 2014.

BCS Noticias. "Antimineros Bloquean Carretera a Todos Santos por Supuesta Aprobación de Los Cardones." *BCS Noticias,* September 23, 2015.

Bizberg, Ilan. "The New Social Movements in Mexico: The Movement for Peace with Justice and Dignity and #YoSoy132." *Foro International,* 55, no.1 (2015).

Bloch, Nadine. "A Spectrum of Allies." In *Beautiful Rising: Creative Resistance from the Global South,* edited by Juman Abujbara, Andrew Boyd, Dave Mitchell and Marcel Taminato. New York/London: Or Books, 2017.

Butcher, J. *Mexican Solidarity, Citizen Participation and Volunteering.* Boston: Springer, 2009.

Cadena, Jorge, ed. *Las Organizaciones Civiles en México Hoy.* Mexico. UNAM, 2004.

Caren, Neal. "Political Process Theory." In *Blackwell Encyclopedia of Sociology*, edited by George Ritzer. Blackwell Publishing, 2007.

Carothers, T., and Brechenmacher, S. *Closing Space: Democracy and Human Rights Support under Fire.* Washington, DC: Carnegie Endowment for International Peace, 2014.

Carvajal, Juan Carlos. "Se Frena Construcción de Presa 'Las Cruces.'" Accessed August 10, 2020. **https://www.grieta.org.mx/index. php/2016/02/29/se-frena-construccion-de-presa-las-cruces/**

CEMDA. "El Pueblo Náyeri y Wixárika Continúan con la Defensa de su Territorio Sagrado contra Proyecto Hidroeléctrico Las Cruces en Nayarit." Accessed June 13, 2017. **https://www.cemda.org.mx/el-pueblo-nayeri-y-wixarika-continuan-con-la-defensa-de-su-territorio-sagrado-contra-proyecto-hidroelectrico-las-cruces-en-nayarit/**

Chenoweth, Erica, and Maria Stephan. *Why Civil Resistance Works: The Strategic Logic of Nonviolent Conflict.* New York: Columbia University Press, 2011.

Cohen, Jean L. and Andrew Arato. *Civil Society and Political Theory.* Cambridge, MA: Massachusetts Institute of Technology, 1992.

Cordero, Laura. "Líder Indígena, Opositor de Hidroeléctrica, da Discurso en DF y en Nayarit lo 'Levantan.'" *Sin Embargo,* December 24, 2014.

Crossman, Ashley. "Political Process Theory: An Overview of the Core Theory of Social Movements." Accessed November 12, 2019. **https://www.thoughtco.com/political-process-theory-3026451**

AIDA. "Entregamos 49 Mil Firmas en la Semarnat: ¡Gracias!," Accessed August 15, 2020. **https://defiendemuxatena.wordpress.com/2014/06/27/entrega-firmas-semarnat-rio-san-pedro-muxatena-change/**

Del Castillo, Augustín. "Coastal Wetlands at Risk." *Meloncoyote* 2, no. 1 (Winter 2011).

Del Castillo, Augustín. "Acusan a la CFE y Nayarit de "Engaños e Intimidación." *Milenio,* December 19, 2013.

Del Castillo, Augustín. "Indígenas de Nayarit Rechazan Proyecto Hidroeléctrico de Las Cruces." *Milenio,* February 19, 2014.

Dominguez Serrano, Judith, ed. *Agua y Territorios: Derechos de los Ciudadanos y Organizaciones Administrativos.* Mexico: Instituto Mexicano de Tecnologia del Agua, 2013.

Dudouet, Véronique. *Powering to Peace: Integrated Civil Resistance and Peacebuilding Strategies.* Washington, DC: ICNC special report, 2017.

Durand, Jorge, ed. *Movimientos sociales.* Guadalajara: Universidad de Guadalajara, 2002.

Edwards, Bob, and John D. McCarthy. "Resources and Social Movement Mobilization." In *The Blackwell Companion to Social Movements,* edited by David A. Snow, Sarah A. Soule, and Hanspeter Kriesi. Oxford: Blackwell Publishing, 2004.

El Universal. "Presentan Plhino para Combatir Crisis Alimentaria." *Vanguardia,* September 4, 2008.

Flores-Márquez, D. "Networks, Social Movements and the Internet in Mexico." Accessed March 21, 2021. **https://www.opendemocracy.net/en/networks-social-movements-and-internet-in-mexico/**

Forbes. "#122 Ricardo Salinas Pliego & Family." Accessed June 2, 2019. **https://www.forbes.com/profile/ricardo-salinas-pliego/#1f0b2b4f1346**

Ganz, Marshall. *Why David Sometimes Wins: Leadership, Organization and Strategy in the California Farm Worker Movement.* New York: Oxford University Press, 2009.

Garcia, Luis Rico, "Building Ties, Social Capital Network Analysis of a Forest Community in a Biosphere Reserve in Chiapas Mexico." *Resistance Alliance,* 2012

Gaxiola, "Nada que ver con Walmart Asegura CEMDA." *Peninsulardigital.com*, April 26, 2013.

Goldberg, Alison D. "Social Change Philanthropy and How It's Done." Accessed March 27, 2020. **https://iawf.org/wp-content/uploads/2013/07/Social-Change-Philanthropy-and-How-It.pdf**

Golder Associates Inc. *Environmental and Social Due Diligence Review: Topolobampo 2200 MTPD Ammonia Plant,* State of Sinaloa, Mexico. Golder Associates, 2016.

Gonzales, M. and M. Guadalupe. "Movimientos Sociales y Desarrollo en México Contemporáneo." *Espacios Públicos* 17, no.39, (April 2015) 93-104.

Gonzalez de Molina, Manuel and Victor M. Toledo. "A Framework for Material Resources." Adapted from the *Social Metabolism.* Switzerland: Springer, 2014.

Gonzalez Lefft, Carlos. "Advierten Afectaciones por Presa Las Cruces." *Meridiano.mx*, February 27, 2019.

Goodwin, J. and J.M. Jasper. *Rethinking Social Movements: Structure, Meaning and Emotions.* Lanham, Maryland: Rowman & Littlefield, 2004.

Guerra Blanco, E. "¿Organizaciones o Movimientos Sociales? Esbozo de una Crítica a una Distinción Conceptual. El Caso de las Organizaciones Sociales en la Ciudad de México." *Territorios,* no. 31 (2014) 15-35.

Merriman, Hardy. "Defining What a Movement Is." *A Movement-Centered Support Model: Considerations for Human Rights Funders and Organizations, Part I.* Accessed December 9, 2019. **https://www.nonviolent-conflict.org/blog_post/movement-centered-support-model-considerations-funders-organizations/**

Holloway, John. *Agrietar el Capitalismo.* Buenos Aires: Ediciones Herramienta, 2011.

Ibarra Meza, Carlos G. *Resistencia al Extractivismo Minero. Una Respuesta a la Mercantilización de Baja California Sur (2009-2018).* PhD diss., Autonomous University of Baja California Sur, 2019.

Jenkins, J. Craig. "Social Movement Philanthropy and the Growth of Nonprofit Political Advocacy: Scope, Legitimacy, and Impact." In *Exploring Organizations and Advocacy: Strategies and Finances* edited by Elizabeth Reid and Maria D. Montilla. Washington, DC: Urban Institute, 2001.

La Jornada. "Los Cardones, Punta de Lanza de la Minería Tóxica en Sierra de la Laguna." *La Jornada,* April 3, 2016.

Layton, M.D. "Philanthropy and the Third Sector in Mexico: The Enabling Environment and its Limitations." *Norteamerica Revista Academica* 4, no. 1, (2009) 87-120.

Loeza, Laura and María Pérez. "La Sociedad Civil Frente a la Militarización de la Seguridad Pública en México." In *Nueva Sociedad*, no. 227, (May/June 2010) 136-152.

Manosmita, M. C. Aruna and K. Libina. "Beyond Resource Mobilization Theory: Dynamic Paradigm of Chengara Struggle." *Journal of Sociology and Social Anthropology* 3, no. 1 (2012) 29-35.

MAPDER. "Realizarán Encuentro Nacional en Defensa del Río San Pedro Mezquital, Nayarit." Accessed March 21, 2021. **http://www.mapder.lunasexta.org/?p=2037**

MAS. "Media Ambiente y Sociedad (MAS)." Accessed June 6, 2019. **http://medioambientebcs.blogspot.com/**

McAdam, D. *Political Process and the Development of Black Insurgency.* Chicago: University of Chicago Press, 1982.

McCarthy, John D. and Mayer N. Zald. "Resource Mobilization and Social Movements: A Partial Theory." *The American Journal of Sociology* 82, no. 6 (May 1977) 1212-1241.

Medina, Elias P. "Gana Amparo Los Cardones," *Sudcaliforniano*, September 10, 2018,

Mejia en la Paz, Pedro Juarez. "Ambientalistas y Políticos de BCS Contra la Minera Paredones Amarillos," *Cronica.com.mx,* January 17, 2010.

Méndez, Ernesto. "Proyecto Hidroeléctrico Amenaza Tierras Sagradas." *Excelsior*, March 1, 2014

Méndez, Ernesto. "Alertan por Proyecto Hidroeléctrico en Nayarit: Advierte que Obra Las Cruces sería Violatoria de Leyes Nacionales e Internacionales." *Compartir Siguenos*, September 27, 2014

Merriman, Hardy. "The trifecta of civil resistance: unity, planning, discipline." Accessed July 16, 2019. **https://www.opendemocracy.net/en/trifecta-of-civil-resistance-unity-planning-discipline/**

Mestries, F., G. Pleyers and S. Zermeño, eds. *Los Movimientos Sociales. De lo local a lo global.* Barcelona: Anthropos, 2009.

Mexico News Daily. "Jalisco's New Governor Announces Santiago River Clean-up." *Mexico News Daily,* December 10, 2018.

Moctezuma, P. "Community-Based Organization and Participatory Planning in South East Mexico City." *Environment and Urbanization* 13, No 2 (October 2001).

Modonesi, Massimo, Lucio Oliver, Fernando Munguía Galeana and Mariana López de la Vega. "México 2000-2009: una década de resistencia popular." In *Una Década en Movimiento. Luchas Populares en América Latina en el Amanecer del Siglo XXI*, edited by Massimo Modonesi and Julién Rebón. Buenos Aires, CLACSO, 2011.

Muñoz Ramírez, Gloria. "#YoSoy132 Voces del Movimiento." Mexico City: Ediciones Bola de Cristal, 2012.

Olson, Georgiana. "Mineras dan Espejitos por Tierras a Ejidatarios." *Excelsior,* May 16, 2011.

Olson, Mancur. *The Logic of Collective Action*. Cambridge, MA: Harvard University Press, 1971.

Palacios Canudas, Ana Elda, "#YoSoy132: Desarrollo y Permanencia: Perspectivas desde la Zona Metropolitana." Masters thesis, El Colegio de México, 2013.

Todos Santos Assemblea Popular, "Pacto de Todos Santos." Accessed March 21, 2021. **www.facebook.com/frenteaguayvidabcs/photos/pcb.568198699973671/568189023307972/**

Pérez, Nahum, "El Mitin de la Estela de Luz: #YoSoy132 se Masifica." *Revista Hashtag* 1, no 4, (May-June 2013) 16.

Pleyers, G. "Autonomías Locales y Subjetividades en contra del Neoliberalismo: hacia un Nuevo Paradigma para entender los Movimientos Sociales." In *Los movimientos sociales. De lo local a lo global,* edited by F. Mestries, G. Pleyers and S. Zermeño. Barcelona: Anthropos, 2009.

Pleyers, G. "El Altermundismo en México. Actores, Culturas Políticas y Prácticas contra el Neoliberalismo." In *Los grandes problemas de México, Tomo VI, Movimientos Sociales,* edited by Ilán Bizberg y Francisco Zapata. Mexico: El Colegio de México, 2010.

Pskowski, Martha. "Hundreds of Unexpected Species found in Mexican UNESCO Site Slated for Gold Mine." *Mongabay,* August 5, 2016.

RECUERDA Video. "SOS Humano en Protesta a las Empresas Canadienses." Accessed March 20, 2021. https://www.facebook.com/watch/?v=196634000362079

Revista Memoria. "Luchas y Movimientos Sociales en México in Revista de Critica Militante." *Revista Memoria* (2019) 67. Accessed March 21, 2021. https://revistamemoria.mx/?p=672

Robinson, Lorin R. "Mining History will Apparently not Repeat itself in Baja California Sur." *Mexico News Daily,* March 22, 2019.

Rodriguez, Carlos Rafael Rea, Luz Angélica Ceballos Chávez and Bertha Alicia Villaseñor Palacios. "Sustainable Balance and Social Resistance in the Watershed of San Pedro River in Nayarit." *Descatos* 47 (January/April 2015).

Santillán, María Luisa. "Movimientos Sociales: Acción Colectiva y Transformadora." Especial México 68. UNAM. 2019. Accessed March 20, 2021. http://ciencia.unam.mx/leer/789/especial-mexico-68-movimientos-sociales-accion-colectiva-y-transformadora

SDPNoticias. "A 4 años: ¿Por qué Desapareció el Activista Antiminero David Sosa?." *SDPNoticias,* December 22, 2015.

Semarnat. *Autorización en Materia de Impacto Ambiental con Resolutivo de Impacto Ambiental No. SGPA/DGIRA/DG/03576 de fecha 21 de Abril del 2014.* Mexico: Semarnat, April 21, 2014.

SinEmbargo. "Hidroeléctrica Las Cruces Violó 6 Tratados Internacionales: los Wixárika se van a los Tribunals," *SinEmbargo.mx,* April 6, 2018,

Somoselmedia. "Hidroeléctrica Las Cruces no es Viable Hoy, ni a Futuro; Revela Nuevo Studio," *Somoselmedia,* February 27, 2019.

Tarrow, Sydney. *The New Transnational Activism.* Cambridge, UK: Cambridge University Press, 2005.

Tilly, Charles. *Social Movements, 1768-2008.* Boulder, London: Paradigm Publishers, 2004.

Torres, Miguel Angel. "Foreign Mining Operations Soundly Rejected." *Meloncoyote* (Winter 2011).

Turak, Natasha. "More than 100 Politicians have been Murdered in Mexico ahead of Sunday's Election," *CNBC,* June 26, 2018.

Walker, E.T. "Beyond Channeling and Professionalization: Foundations as Strategic Players." In *Players and Arenas: The Interactive Dynamics of Protest.* Amsterdam: Amsterdam University Press, 2015.

YoSoy132. "Principios Generales del Movimiento." Accessed March 21, 2021. https://www.scribd.com/document/101496747/Principios-Generales-Del-Movimiento-YoSoy132

Zapata, F. *El Sindicalismo Latinoamericano.* Mexico City: El Colegio de México, 2013.

Zaragoza, M.A., ed. *Movimientos Sociales en Mexico Apuntos Teoricos y Estudios de Caso.* Mexico City: UNAM, 2016.

About the Authors

A. Scott DuPree (PhD, Civil Society Transitions) has worked for 30 years in helping build and strengthen social and environmental initiatives in Southern Africa, Brazil, Mexico, Southeast Asia and the United States. Scott holds a PhD in international affairs focused on the dynamic role of civil society. He has assisted international organizations and philanthropic foundations to advance civic approaches to development, human rights, the environment and grassroots activism. Scott was regional director for Africa for The Synergos Institute, co-founder and Program Director for Conectas Direitos Humanos, Greengrants Alliance coordinator for Global Greengrants Fund and the principal of Civil Society Transitions through which he has consulted for numerous organizations around the world. Scott is also a professor in the Master's of Development program "Global Classroom" at Regis University where he teaches participatory planning and grassroots and indigenous activism.

Chris Allan, Ajabu Advisors LLC, has experience with public donors, foundations, and local and international NGOs working in social change, including designing, planning, implementing, and evaluating programs around the globe. He has led or participated in evaluations of global networks, international partnerships, and organizations in many countries (including Brazil, Georgia, Ghana, Indonesia, Kyrgyzstan, Mexico, Niger, Peru, Russia, Rwanda, Somalia, Sudan, Tajikistan, Tanzania, and Zimbabwe). In the human rights field, he has organized and funded grassroots groups, national coalitions, and global alliances working on public participation in decision making about a wide range of issues. He has set up and led grantmaking programs in East Africa, Southern Africa, and globally. He holds a master's degree in Social Change and Development from The Johns Hopkins University School of Advanced International Studies, and a Bachelor's Degree from Wesleyan University in African Studies and Biology.